RABBI KIRT A. SCHNEIDER

ENTERING *His* PRESENCE

CHARISMA HOUSE

Visit the author's website at discoveringthejewishjesus.com.

Cataloging-in-Publication Data is on file with the Library of Congress.
International Standard Book Number: 978-1-63641-172-9
E-book ISBN: 978-1-63641-173-6

23 24 25 26 27 — 987654321
Printed in the United States of America

CONTENTS

~~~

INTRODUCTION

MANY OF YOU know my story, but permit me to take just a few paragraphs to share it for the benefit of those who are not familiar with the way I came to faith. I came to faith in 1978. As a Jewish person, I knew nothing about Jesus. No one had ever witnessed to me. I had never read the New Testament. Jesus was as far away from me as the man on the moon. I'd never thought about Jesus or even considered Him.

Then, one day when I was twenty years old, I was supernaturally awakened in the middle of the night, and Yeshua (Jesus) appeared to me in a vision. He was on the cross. Everything around Him was in vivid color, and a ray of red light shot straight down through the sky onto Jesus' head. I knew the person on the cross was Jesus. But when I saw that beam of red light shining down on Yeshua's head, I knew the light was coming from God, and I knew He was saying to me, "Jesus is the way to Me." Then, suddenly, I woke up.

The vision lasted no more than a few seconds, but I knew God had just revealed Himself to me. After that experience, I started telling everybody about Yeshua—and after more than forty years, I haven't stopped!

Perhaps because I came to faith through a supernatural encounter with Jesus, I have been on a quest to experience more and more of God's presence in my life ever since. My goal as a believer has been to enter into deeper and deeper realms in God's Spirit. I want to move His heart and see His glory manifest in my life. I'm not after religion. I want to know God. I don't want to just memorize scriptures. I don't want to simply know *about* God. I want to experience Him. I want to be aware of His presence. I want a deep, intimate connection with my Creator.

So many people are looking to the world to satisfy them. They seek the comfort of material things, the applause of their peers, or likes and follows on social media to meet their deep need for connection. But Yeshua said, "Whoever drinks of the water that I will give him shall never thirst; but the water that I will give him will become in him a well of water springing up to eternal life."[1] To truly fill the void in our souls, we must enter God's presence and experience His reality, and the great news is there is always more of Him to discover.

Beloved one, this is my heart's passion. I want to get a tighter and tighter hold on the Lord and know more and more of His reality in my life. Thus, in the pages that follow, I offer keys for entering into an authentic relationship with Yeshua that will empower us not only to receive answers to our prayers but also to connect with God in a deeper intimacy.

In the first part of this book, I lay a foundation for entering God's presence by sharing how we can go before the Lord in authentic prayer and walk in supernatural unity with Him. Spending time with God was never meant to be an obligation; rather, it is an opportunity to experience oneness with our Creator. We are called not to a religious routine but to a relationship with a loving Father who is alive, hears us, and wants to make Himself known to us.

That section is followed by one hundred daily

devotionals you can use to put this teaching into practice. Each devotional focuses on a verse or passage of Scripture because walking with God is about walking in His Word. Yeshua said the Father is looking for those who will worship Him *in spirit and truth*.[2] Our relationship with God is based on both the Word and the Spirit.

Our relationship with God was never meant to be relegated to the mind. Father God wants to connect with us in our *kishkes*, in the depths of our insides, and empower us to live out our divine purpose and destiny from that place of intimacy.

Yeshua said, "He who believes in Me, as the Scripture said, 'From his innermost being will flow rivers of living water.'"[3] Jesus wants to become a well of living water springing up from *within us* to eternal life. This is the truth that should mark our lives. We can know God and His love for us. We can feel His glory and experience His power. We can walk in supernatural oneness with our Father and Creator. Let's keep pressing in to Jesus!

A NOTE ABOUT TERMINOLOGY

Throughout this book, you will find that I use various Hebrew terms to refer to God, Jesus, and the Holy Spirit.

Occasionally I use the name Yahweh when referring to God. Yahweh is God's covenant name that He revealed to His people in Exodus 6:3. It is often translated "LORD" in the Old Testament.

Another name I use for God is HaShem, which is translated in English as "The Name." Within the culture of Judaism there is a sense that God is so holy that His actual name is not pronounced, so He is referred to simply as HaShem ("The Name").

In addition to these, I use other Hebrew terms that may already be familiar to you, including Yeshua (Jesus) and the Ruach HaKodesh (Holy Spirit).

Chapter 1

AUTHENTIC COMMUNION
WITH GOD

So many people want a deeper relationship with God. They want to feel His presence and experience His reality on a daily basis. But they don't know where to begin. The reality is that just as natural relationships are built and nurtured through communication, so is our relationship with HaShem. Thus, moving into deeper realms in God first involves going deeper in conversation with Him through prayer.

When a lot of people think of prayer, they associate it with works. They think of prayer as something they have to know how to do. They feel pressure to pray "correctly," as if there's one right way to commune with God.

In reality, true prayer—what I call authentic prayer—has nothing to do with religion or following a formula. In fact, I don't even like to use the words *prayer* and *religion* in the same sentence because religion has nothing to do with developing true communion with God.

Studies have shown that people are happier when they're authentic in their relationships—when they are genuine, transparent, focused, and fully present in their interactions.[1] The same is true of our relationship with God. If we're going to enter into deeper realms of God's presence, if we're going to move His heart and see His glory manifest in our lives, then we can't speak to Him superficially out of a sense of obligation. We can't say certain words because we think that's what we're supposed to do. To truly connect with the Lord in prayer,

1

we have to speak to Him from our hearts. Our connection to Him has to be real.

Let's face it, many of us have bowed our heads, perhaps before a meal, and said religious words when in reality our hearts were not connected to God. Jesus accused the Pharisees of this. He said, "This people honors Me with their lips, but their heart is far away from Me."[2] They performed many religious deeds, but the reality is their hearts and minds were not really connected to God.

God is not calling us to a religious routine. God created you and me in His own image so we could walk with Him and know Him. We were created to be in relationship, to experience His glory, and to return the love He has given us. That's really what prayer is. Prayer is about creating a deep, intimate connection between our Creator and us so we can live in our divine purpose and destiny. But how do we develop this kind of relationship with God?

AUTHENTIC PRAYER BEGINS WITH FAITH

Authentic prayer starts with faith. The Bible says in Hebrews 11:6 that "without faith it is impossible to please Him, for he who comes to God must believe that He is and that He is a rewarder of those who seek Him." This tells us that the first step in communicating with God in a real, authentic way is to believe that He exists. After all, how would we be motivated to talk with someone we don't believe is listening? Why would we cry out to someone we don't think would respond?

Developing a relationship with God that draws us into living and authentic prayer begins with faith—with believing that God exists.

And then the writer of Hebrews says we must believe that "He is a rewarder of those who diligently seek Him." This means we must believe that if we call upon Him, He's going to answer us. This really is the foundation for authentic prayer—believing there is a God, that He hears us, and that as we call out to Him, He responds.

Of course, this doesn't mean that every time we ask God for something, we're going to see something happen immediately. God's ways are not our ways, and a thousand years to us is like one day to the Lord. He answers in His own way and in His own time. But authentic prayer happens when we believe that God exists and that He does respond.

Believing God hears you when you pray creates a momentum for you to enter into communion and communication with Him. If you and I deep in our hearts know there's a Creator, are desperate for answers, and are hungry to know Him and experience His presence— we're going to call out to Him in prayer. People who are trapped in darkness, who have lost a vision for the reality of God in the earth, are not going to talk to Him, but I trust that this is not you.

AUTHENTIC PRAYER IS GENUINE

This brings me to the next truth about authentic prayer: it's genuine. When we're praying authentically, we're calling upon God from our hearts without putting on any type of persona.

Sometimes when people pray, they suddenly change their voice, their tone, and even their language. They begin to speak in *thees* and *thous*: "Oh great and mighty One, to Thee we pray..." This type of language doesn't necessarily get God's attention. God responds when we are being genuine and transparent with Him and speak to Him from our hearts as we would talk to our trusted best friend.

Consider this: the Lord knows everything about you and me. He knows the vile attitudes we have sometimes. He knows the jealousy, the selfishness, even the hatred we experience in our hearts at times. He knows all that. But the Bible says that while we were yet sinners, Christ died for us.[3] If Jesus died for us when we were living completely separated from God, how much more can we trust Him to love and accept us now that we're focusing our attention on Him?

The Bible tells us to come boldly before the throne of grace.[4] Despite our sin, despite our imperfection, despite the things in our souls that need to be cleansed, we can come boldly to God *just as we are* because of the blood of Jesus. We can have confidence that we can be transparent with the Lord. The enemy perverts people's thinking and makes them afraid to come to God because they feel sinful. That's what the enemy wants. He wants people to feel trapped in their guilt so they'll be intimidated to talk to God.

This is what happened to Adam and Eve in the Garden of Eden. The Bible tells us in the Book of Bereshit, or Genesis, that after Adam and Eve sinned, they suddenly realized they were naked. Before they sinned, they were God conscious, but after they sinned, their connection to the Lord was broken. They lost that God conscious-ness, and instead, their attention was turned to focus on themselves. They became self-conscious, and in that state of self-consciousness, they felt insecure and afraid. They suddenly felt naked, and they began to run from God.

> The LORD God commanded the man, saying, "From any tree of the garden you may eat freely; but from the tree of the knowledge of good and evil you shall not eat, for in the day that you eat from it you will surely die."…
>
> Now the serpent was more crafty than any beast of the field which the LORD God had made. And he said to the woman, "Indeed, has God said, 'You shall not eat from any tree of the garden'?" The woman said to the serpent, "From the fruit of the trees of the garden we may eat; but from the fruit of the tree which is in the middle of the garden, God has said, 'You shall not eat from it or touch it, or you will die.'" The serpent said to the woman, "You surely will not die! For God knows that in the day you eat from it your eyes will be

opened, and you will be like God, knowing good and evil."

When the woman saw that the tree was good for food, and that it was a delight to the eyes, and that the tree was desirable to make one wise, she took from its fruit and ate; and she gave also to her husband with her, and he ate. Then the eyes of both of them were opened, and they knew that they were naked; and they sewed fig leaves together and made themselves loin coverings.

They heard the sound of the Lord God walking in the garden in the cool of the day, and the man and his wife hid themselves from the presence of the Lord God among the trees of the garden.[5]

Humanity is in the same plight today, but people don't realize it. They're running from a sense of their guilt and from God. Like Adam and Eve, humanity is still trying to cover up their nakedness. We're trying to cover up our feeling inside that something's not right, that anxiousness that comes from not being connected to Father God. We try to cover that sense of anxiety, that sense of guilt, that sense of shame by putting things over our lives. Whether it's social media, illicit relationships, food, alcohol, or something else, we're doing the same thing Adam and Eve did when they attempted to run and hide from God—we're looking for something to cover our nakedness.

So the key is to not let the enemy make us feel ashamed. We need to come to God just as we are, knowing that despite our sin, we're "accepted in the Beloved."[6] When we know that Jesus loves us—*really* know, in our heart of hearts—we can be open and completely transparent with Him. The key to authentic prayer is to simply talk to God transparently.

It might sound like this: "Father God, I'm feeling really bad inside. I feel yucky. I don't know what's wrong, but I feel afraid. I feel lonely. I feel like my heart is defiled."

Whatever you're feeling, you can talk to God about it. You can go to Him transparently, right where you are. If you're struggling in sin, you can cry out to God in the midst of your sin. You can talk to Him about it just as you talk to yourself about it, and when you talk to Him about it, He enters into that place of need. But this will only happen when you're being open and transparent.

One of the fundamental truths of the kingdom is that God's power is perfected in our weakness.[7] When we depend upon the Lord, when we're in a state of weakness, His grace comes in and strengthens us, propelling us into future momentum and breakthrough. Rather than letting the challenge you're facing make you run from God because you're ashamed of it, or letting it make you fearful and anxious so you shut yourself off from communion with Him, connect with Him in your challenge. And have faith that the challenge can actually be turned into a gift to you from God, because man's problems are God's opportunities!

Rather than looking at your challenge as something terrible, embrace it. Thank God for it. As you connect with the Lord and depend on Him in the midst of your challenge, you'll be brought into union with Him through Yeshua and you will be strengthened because His power will be perfected in your weakness. You will eventually overcome it, and a fusion will take place in your soul as you walk through that trial depending on God.

In 2 Corinthians 12, Paul tells us he was dealing with some type of torment that was being caused by what he called "a messenger of Satan." Paul also revealed that this challenge in his life was part of God's plan: "Because of the surpassing greatness of the revelations, for this reason, to keep me from exalting myself, there was given me a thorn in the flesh, a messenger of Satan to torment me—to keep me from exalting myself!"[8] In other words, the Lord was behind this satanic attack. What the enemy meant for evil, God was architecting for good. I know this is a strong statement, and many may find it hard to digest. But read Paul's words again. The Lord's purpose was to guard Paul from pride and to keep him depending on Him.

Paul went on to say, "Concerning this I implored the Lord three times that it might leave me. And He has said to me, 'My grace is sufficient for you, for power is perfected in weakness.' Most gladly, therefore, I will rather boast about my weaknesses, so that the power of Christ may dwell in me."[9]

Consider again that the Scriptures say three times Paul cried out, "Lord, take away this problem, this messenger of Satan." We don't know what the issue was, but it was causing Paul pain. Finally, after calling upon the Lord three times, Paul heard the Lord say, "Paul, I'm not going to take the problem away. My grace is sufficient for you to get through this problem. And beyond that, My power will be perfected in your weakness."

The problem was making Paul weak, but in Paul's weakness, he became even more desperate for the Lord. And the Lord said to him, "Through the desperation that you're experiencing because of this overwhelming problem, I'm going to fuse your soul to Mine. You're going to come out of this thing empowered because you depended on Me in your weakness and were made strong."

Beloved one, God's power is made perfect in our weakness, so be transparent with Him. Real prayer takes place when you simply talk to God and share everything with Him. You have to open up to Him and share your life with Him. You can't talk to God just when you're feeling holy. You can't talk to God just when you're at church. Paul said, "Pray without ceasing."[10] That means we talk to God about everything—the good, the bad, and the ugly. When you're struggling, whether it's sin, pride, selfishness, sexual temptation, a foul attitude, a demonic spirit—whatever it is—you talk to God about it. Amen.

He's right with you in it. He wants to unite with you in the valleys. That's where your strength is forged. In 2 Corinthians 1, Paul said, "We do not want you to be unaware, brethren, of our affliction which came to us in Asia, that we were burdened excessively, beyond our strength, so that we despaired even of life."[11]

Paul was so challenged, he was so heavily burdened,

he didn't want to continue on. The weight was that heavy. Please don't misunderstand. Paul obviously did not have a suicidal spirit. He just said life was so hard that in the natural he didn't want to go on. But then he said this: "Indeed, we had the sentence of death within ourselves so that we would not trust in ourselves, but in God who raises the dead."[12]

In other words, Paul was saying, "God has put me in such a place of hardship and weakness that there is no natural help for me. There is nobody who can help me. My doctor can't help me. My parents can't help me. My spouse can't help me. My pastor can't help me. My insurance agent can't help me. My governor can't help me. The president can't help me. Nobody can help me." But then he said in essence, "This all has come upon me so that I would come to the very end of every earthly resource so there's only one thing left to do, and that's to look up and connect with God, who raises the dead."

This is how we enter God's presence through authentic prayer. Jesus said, "Behold, I stand at the door and knock; if anyone hears My voice and opens the door, I will come in to him and will dine with him, and he with Me."[13] Sometimes people hear that scripture quoted when an evangelist gives an invitation for people to accept Yeshua (Jesus) as their Savior for the first time. And that is a very good use of this particular verse. But it means so much more.

The Spirit of the Lord is continually knocking at the door of our hearts every single day because He wants to come into us in a deeper way than we've let Him.

He wants us to surrender to His mastery, His lordship over our lives, more than we have. Transparent prayer is about letting God in, surrendering to Him, and trusting Him. As we do that, we surrender to His lordship and move further into the depths of authentic prayer.

AUTHENTIC PRAYER IS CONTINUAL

In John 11, Jesus made a simple but profound statement. He was just about to raise Lazarus from the dead, and a crowd had gathered around Him. After He told them to move the stone from Lazarus' tomb, He lifted His eyes to heaven and said: "Father, I thank You that You have heard Me. *I knew that You always hear Me*; but because of the people standing around I said it, so that they may believe that You sent Me."[14]

Now, bear in mind that He hadn't said anything yet. There was no preceding prayer. It wasn't as if Jesus had been speaking out loud in prayer before He made this statement. Yeshua said, "I knew that You always hear Me," because He always had an internal dialogue going on with the Spirit in His soul. He walked continually in a silent, internal discourse with the Father. The words and emotions that Yeshua shared with the Father were not always expressed out loud. He lived in a secret place. He lived out of an inward knowing, and He lived from the inside out. When Jesus said, "Father, I thank You that You have heard Me," He was saying, "Father, I'm speaking to You now with My audible voice so everybody around Me will understand our relationship."

We are striving for a continual internal communication with the Spirit of God. The Scriptures say, "Pray without ceasing."[15] Prayer doesn't have to be out loud. We're praying when we're reaching out to God, even if it's simply from our hearts or minds.

The Hebrew word *kavanah* means direction or intention. It is often used in relation to focus and concentration in prayer. When we're directing our focus toward the Lord, when we're desiring Him, that's prayer because prayer is simply reaching out to God. When we're setting our attention on Father God and reaching out to Him in our hearts, we're praying, whether or not an audible word escapes our lips. Beloved one, God hears the most subtle movement of your soul. You don't have to raise your voice and project loudly or use eloquent words for God to hear you. He already hears you.

You don't have to go out "there" somewhere to connect with Him. God is in the center of your heart right now, and He wants you to know He already hears you, whether or not you make a sound.

> It is not in heaven, that you should say, "Who will go up to heaven for us to get it for us and make us hear it, that we may observe it?" Nor is it beyond the sea, that you should say, "Who will cross the sea for us to get it for us and make us hear it, that we may observe it?" But the word is very near you, in your mouth and in your heart, that you may observe it.[16]

Paul proclaimed this same principle of the kingdom: "But the righteousness based on faith speaks as follows: 'Do not say in your heart, "Who will ascend into heaven?" (that is, to bring Christ down), or "Who will descend into the abyss?" (that is, to bring Christ up from the dead).' But what does it say? 'The word is near you, in your mouth and in your heart'—that is, the word of faith which we are preaching."[17]

God the Father longs for us to know that He hears the faintest whisper of our being. Trust Him.

Chapter 2

ENTERING INTO DEEPER INTIMACY

ONE OF THE most authentic prayers in Scripture is in Psalm 51, written by David, the great king of Israel, after he sinned with Bathsheba and had her husband killed. This psalm reveals the transparency, depth, and intimacy of David's relationship with God.

Even though David lived long before Yeshua walked the earth, the psalms show that he had a relationship with Messiah Jesus and was led by the Spirit of God. We see this, for example, in Psalm 110:1, where David writes, "The LORD says to my Lord: 'Sit at My right hand until I make Your enemies a footstool for Your feet.'" The "Lord" David was referring to is Messiah Jesus.

Yeshua even quoted David's words in Psalm 110:1 to the Pharisees when they were trying to trap Him. Jesus asked, "What do you think about the Christ, whose son is He?" The Pharisees answered Him, "The son of David." Yeshua then asked, "Then how does David in the Spirit call Him 'Lord,' saying, 'The Lord said to my Lord, "Sit at My right hand, until I put Your enemies beneath Your feet"'? If David then calls Him 'Lord,' how is He his son?"[1]

The Pharisees didn't know how to respond to that. Somehow David understood a mystery of God's nature that stumped even the religious elite of Jesus' day. So as we prepare to study Psalm 51, let us bear in mind that David, the ancient Hebrew king, knew Messiah Jesus and the psalms were inspired by the Ruach HaKodesh, the Holy Spirit.

In light of this, let's now turn our attention to David's prayer.

Be gracious to me, O God, according to Your lov-ingkindness; according to the greatness of Your compassion blot out my transgressions. Wash me thoroughly from my iniquity and cleanse me from my sin. For I know my transgressions, and my sin is ever before me. Against You, You only, I have sinned and done what is evil in Your sight, so that You are justified when You speak and blameless when You judge. Behold, I was brought forth in iniquity, and in sin my mother conceived me. Behold, You desire truth in the innermost being, and in the hidden part You will make me know wisdom. Purify me with hyssop, and I shall be clean; wash me, and I shall be whiter than snow. Make me to hear joy and gladness, let the bones which You have broken rejoice. Hide Your face from my sins and blot out all my iniquities. Create in me a clean heart, O God, and renew a steadfast spirit within me.[2]

In this chapter and the next, we will look closely at David's words in this psalm because they offer so many insights into how we can become more transparent before God and enter more fully into deep, intimate, authentic prayer.

APPEALING TO THE GOD OF GRACE

David begins by saying, "Be gracious to me, O God, according to Your lovingkindness." The first thing David did is appeal to the God of grace. Paul did the same thing in his letters in the New Testament. He began each one by saying something along the lines of, "Grace and peace to you from God our Father and the Lord Jesus Christ."[3] David was appealing to this same One, asking Him to be gracious.

Why would David begin his prayer this way? It's because of the nature of grace. While grace is many things, one important definition is that it is God's undeserved love and empowerment to be accepted, favored, and loved by Him. Ephesians 2:8 tells us, "By grace you have been saved through faith; and that not of yourselves, it is the gift of God." Grace is God's love extended to us. It involves both God's forgiveness and His empowerment to supernaturally walk with Him and know Him. So David begins his prayer by reaching out to a God who did not reward him according to his sins but who David knew is a God of love.

I want you to stamp that truth on your heart. The God we serve, the God of the Hebrew Bible (the Old Testament) and the Brit Chadashah (the New Testament) is a God who loves and accepts you for who you are, right where you are. This is why the Bible says we've been "accepted in the Beloved."[4] God accepts you right where you are, whoever you are, if you will look to Jesus.

David had confidence that his Creator is a God of

love. David was not perfect. After all, he had sinned with Bathsheba and ordered the murder of her husband. I mean, how much worse does it get? Yet he still had confidence that his God loved him. That's a lesson for you and me.

Of course, this same and identical truth is emphasized in the New Testament. Paul said he was the chief of sinners.[5] Before he became a follower of Yeshua, Paul persecuted the church. He sought to arrest and brutalize any Jew who believed in Jesus, yet God intervened and saved him. The lesson learned from this is that if God would save him while he was arresting Jewish believers, beating them, and putting them in prison, He'll save anybody.[6]

I don't know what you did last night. I don't know what you did this morning. I don't know what fight you might have had with your spouse, what harsh words might have been spoken. I don't know what addictions you might be fighting. I don't know if you're an alcoholic, a drug addict, a sex addict, a television addict—I don't know where you are, but Jesus does, and "it is a trustworthy statement, deserving full acceptance, that Christ Jesus came into the world to save sinners."[7] That's you and me. You can turn to this God of love and grace at any time. David knew that. If you look to Father in Jesus' name, He will receive you. You too can go boldly before the throne of grace. Knowing this is key in entering into deeper communion with God. "Therefore let us draw near with confidence to the throne of grace, so that we may receive mercy and find grace to help in time of need."[8]

David goes on to say, "According to Your loving-kindness; according to the greatness of Your compassion blot out my transgressions."[9] I love David's words in Psalm 103: "He has not dealt with us according to our sins, nor rewarded us according to our iniquities. For as high as the heavens are above the earth, so great is His lovingkindness toward those who fear Him."[10]

This is what Jesus does for you and me. No matter what we've done, through Jesus' blood our sins are forgiven.

We can be confident that we are loved and accepted by our Creator despite anything we've ever thought, spoken, or done because Yeshua's blood has been given for you and me. The Scriptures make it clear that forgiveness is granted when innocent blood has been shed. This is a thread that runs throughout the Hebrew Bible. Some even trace it back to Adam and Eve, when God made them clothing of animal skins after they sinned. Assuming that the skins the Lord clothed Adam and Eve with were made from animals that were alive before they sinned, the blood of those animals had to be shed in order for those skins to be made.

We see this same principle of substitutionary sacrificial atonement through blood clearly illustrated in Yom Kippur, the Day of Atonement, when the high priest took the blood of the bull and the blood of the goat into the Holy of Holies (housed first in the Tabernacle, then later in the Temple). When God looked at the blood the high priest poured over the Ark of the Covenant, He said, "The life of the flesh is in the blood, and I have given it to you on the altar to make atonement for your souls; for it is the blood by reason of the life that makes atonement."[11]

Through the blood of Messiah we can come to God, and He will blot out our sin. David understood this, and we too must understand it if we want to be secure enough to be real before God in prayer. David had committed adultery with Bathsheba and ordered the murder of her husband when he went to the Father and said, "According to the greatness of Your compassion blot out my transgressions." Beloved one, you can go boldly before God too. No matter what you've done, you can ask Him to blot out your transgressions.

Think about this: There are a lot of people who believe in karma. It's the idea based in Eastern religions that whatever you put out there in the world is going to come back to you. Some Eastern religions teach reincarnation—if you're good in this life, you'll come back in the next life as something higher. But if you're bad in this life, you might come back as a turtle, a frog, a lizard, or an ant.

The good news is that when you surrender your life to Yeshua, even if you've done bad things in your past, the curse is broken. You don't have to reap the full consequences of all the evil and sinful deeds you've done because Jesus took your sin and mine in His own body, spilling His blood on our behalf. He delivered us from the torturing power of the enemy. We opened a door to let Satan enter our lives when we sinned, but the blood of Jesus cuts off the devil's accusation. Now we are able to enter through the crucified and risen One into a life of blessing.

I love the way the apostle Paul opens the Book of Ephesians by saying, "Blessed be the God and Father of our Lord Jesus Christ, who has blessed us with every spiritual blessing in the heavenly places in Christ."[12] Yeshua has blessed us. He hasn't cursed us. He's not waiting for something bad to come back on you. Messiah Jesus stopped that. He reversed the curse. Yeshua put up a blood wall blocking the penalty of your sin. In Him now, you have been blessed "with every spiritual blessing in the heavenly places."

We must believe this if we are to have the confidence we need to open up to God in authentic prayer. We must know that in Yeshua we are loved, accepted, and treasured.

Once David had the confidence in God's love for him to come into His presence, knowing he was loved despite his sin, he asked God to sanctify him. David says in verses 2 and 3 of Psalm 51, "Wash me thoroughly from my iniquity and cleanse me from my sin. For I know my transgressions, and my sin is ever before me."

We come to our Creator knowing we are clean in the blood of Jesus, asking HaShem to rewire our minds and hearts to bring us into alignment with His holiness so we can know Him and walk with Him. We say, "Father, wash me from the defilement that my sin has left me with." This process is called sanctification.

A HUMBLE HEART

Even the apostle Paul was still striving to overcome evil. This kept him humble. He realized that he was forever dependent on God's mercy and help. He wrote in the Book of Romans:

> I know that nothing good dwells in me, that is, in my flesh; for the willing is present in me, but the doing of the good is not. For the good that I want, I do not do, but I practice the very evil that I do not want. But if I am doing the very thing I do not want, I am no longer the one doing it, but sin which dwells in me....Wretched man that I am! Who will set me free from the body of this death? Thanks be to God through Jesus Christ our Lord![13]

Like David and Paul, we connect with God through a humble heart, looking for mercy. We don't come in a religious spirit. Some people pray so as to be seen praying. We need to guard our hearts from this, especially when praying out loud with others present. That's what Jesus accused the Pharisees of. He said, "You guys say these long, religious prayers, thinking God is going to respond because of your many words. But you do everything to be noticed by men."[14]

Rather than praying out of a humble heart, when we're in church or with Christian friends, we sometimes don't realize we're really focusing on how religious and sanctified we sound to the people around us instead of truly talking to God. We have to break off this demonic, defiled mindset. It doesn't matter what anybody thinks. We don't do what we do to be noticed by men. Authentic prayer requires a humble heart that is focused on Jesus and the Father, not ourselves.

In Exodus 25 the Lord told Moses He wanted him to build a Tabernacle, which in Hebrew is called a *Mishkan*. The Lord wanted this Tabernacle, this *Mishkan*, because He desired to meet with His people there and dwell with them: "Let them construct a sanctuary for Me, that I may dwell among them."[15] So the *Mishkan* gives us insight into how to enter His presence.

The Lord told Moses, "According to all that I am going to show you, as the pattern of the tabernacle and the pattern of all its furniture, just so you shall construct it."[16] Every piece of the Tabernacle, which later became the Temple in Jerusalem, was constructed through a divine blueprint, and every part of it has meaning that teaches us how to have fellowship with the Lord. As we flow with the spiritual principles it reveals, God is able to make His home with us.

When you entered the Tabernacle, you entered a room called the Holy Place. That room was completely concealed with animal skins, both its sides and roof, so no wind was able to enter. It was totally cut off from the light of the natural world. The only light in the room was through a seven-branched menorah that was continuously burning. This is symbolic of the Holy Spirit and teaches us that we must live not by the natural light of the sun but by the supernatural light of God's Spirit.

Again, there was no natural light in the Tabernacle. There was only the supernatural light from the menorah.

> "For My thoughts are not your thoughts, nor are your ways My ways," declares the Lord. "For as the heavens are higher than the earth, so are My ways higher than your ways and My thoughts than your thoughts."[17]

Also inside the Holy Place within the Tabernacle, there was an Altar of Incense continuously burning. The incense represents the prayers of the saints.[18]

Remember, no natural wind could get in the room because it was completely covered with animal skins. This means that as the incense was burning, the smoke ascended straight up because there was no wind to blow it horizontally. If I were to burn incense while standing outside, the smoke of that incense would not go straight up because the wind would blow it sideways. It would go off sideward in whatever direction the wind was blowing.

But in the Tabernacle, the smoke went straight up. It ascended right to HaShem, to Father God. This is what true, authentic prayer does. It ascends straight up to God. Unfortunately, many of our prayers that we pray in Jesus' name do not ascend straight up to God. They're blowing to the side toward the people next to us because we're more focused on impressing those around us. Sometimes we may be more focused on making a good religious impression on the people around us than we are on actually talking to God. This pretense of prayer, beloved one, has to stop.

If we want to be heard by the Lord in such a way that He responds with joy to our prayers, if we want to move His heart, we need to be humble and sincere. We need to recognize that we're standing in God's presence. We need to talk to Him without trying to impress others.

David was aware that he was standing before God alone. His prayer ascended straight up. He said, "Against You, You only, I have sinned and done what is evil in Your sight, so that You are justified when You speak and blameless when You judge."[19]

Beloved one, let's go before the Lord in humility and sincerity. Let's have godly fear. Let's be more conscious of His presence than of ourselves or others. Let's be confident in His blood, that we are forgiven, accepted, treasured, and loved. Let's ask Him to cleanse and wash us of all defilement. And let's purpose to not sin against Him.

Chapter 3

LIVING FROM THE INSIDE OUT

As we continue to study his prayer in Psalm 51, David moves us into an even deeper understanding of authentic communion and communication with God. Again, David prayed:

> Be gracious to me, O God, according to Your lovingkindness; according to the greatness of Your compassion blot out my transgressions. Wash me thoroughly from my iniquity and cleanse me from my sin. For I know my transgressions, and my sin is ever before me. Against You, You only, I have sinned and done what is evil in Your sight, so that You are justified when You speak and blameless when You judge. Behold, I was brought forth in iniquity, and in sin my mother conceived me. Behold, You desire truth in the innermost being, and in the hidden part You will make me know wisdom. Purify me with hyssop, and I shall be clean; wash me, and I shall be whiter than snow. Make me to hear joy and gladness, let the bones which You have broken rejoice. Hide Your face from my sins and blot out all my iniquities. Create in me a clean heart, O God, and renew a steadfast spirit within me.[1]

Notice David's words in verse 6: "Behold, You desire truth in the innermost being, and in the hidden part You will make me know wisdom." Think for a minute about what this verse is actually saying. The Lord wants to connect with us in the innermost part of our souls.

But how many of us are even aware of our innermost being? How many of us are so connected to the outer world that we're not in touch with who we are on the inside?

Eternal life spreads from the inside out, and that's how God wants us to live—from the inside out. He wants to draw us back into our innermost beings. But as I said in a previous chapter, ever since Adam and Eve disobeyed God, people have been running from themselves. After Adam and Eve sinned, the first thing they did was run from God and from themselves. Why? Because they felt such guilt, insecurity, and shame inside.

Ever since Adam and Eve's fall in the garden, people have been in a plight of running from themselves and from God. But the only way for us to be fulfilled is to stop running, to stop trying to cover up that nakedness, that guilt, that insecurity that plagues humanity, and instead practice just sitting before God. This reminds me of a vision of the night I had several years ago.

Although I was maintaining my spiritual discipline of sitting before the Lord each day, there were times when it became difficult. During this time, God encouraged me through His Spirit in a dream. I was in a little one-room cabin. In the middle of the room was a simple wooden table, and on the other side of it sat a man who I sensed was a familiar friend, but I didn't recognize him. I also sensed I had been there for some time, and I was feeling antsy. I looked out the window of this cabin, saw the beautiful natural scenery, and wanted to go out of the cabin and do something. I thought, "I have been sitting here long enough. It's time for me to get out of here." I was on the edge of standing up and leaving when I heard a voice say, "That man sitting across from you, who feels like a familiar friend, is Jesus. Just keep sitting across from Him, and you'll be made whole."

What I believe the Lord was telling me was to continue to practice sitting before Him in stillness. He was saying, "Don't run away when you get restless and uncomfortable or your mind tells you there is something else you should be doing. Believe in the process, even when it feels as if nothing is happening and you're bored and fidgety. Continue to face Me and allow Me to bring to the surface what I need to heal so I can ground you in Me and make you complete."

The Lord says, "Be still, and know that I am God."[2] In order to know God and get in touch with what David called the innermost being, we have to practice being still. This involves fasting from the things in the outer world that distract us from Him. We have to turn off the phone, the television, the noise in our lives, and quiet ourselves. As we still our hearts in God's presence, He will soften our hearts so we can better discern His voice and the gentle leading of His Spirit. We will receive an impartation.

David said, "Surely I have composed and quieted my soul; like a weaned child rests against his mother, my soul is like a weaned child within me."[3] Sadly, many of us can't be still. We need our phones in hand, and we're constantly watching for new notifications. It's amazing to me how the devil has so succeeded in capturing people through their smartphones. Everywhere you look, people are walking around connected to that smartphone all day long, constantly being drawn outside themselves to seek some type of satisfaction from the outer world. Studies have shown that smartphone activity causes our brains to release dopamine, the same chemical that makes us feel happy, motivated, or aroused.[4]

We get a little high from using our smartphones, as if there's some kind of answer in the latest text or social media post. There's no answer there. You may be familiar with studies that have corroborated the fact that the more time people spend on social media, the more depressed they become.[5] Why? Because when we look to the world for satisfaction, we always end up disappointed. We keep hoping that we will find fulfillment in the pseudo world of social media, but we always come up empty-handed and as a result are sad.

We are looking for life where there is no life: "For My people have committed two evils: they have forsaken Me, the fountain of living waters, to hew for themselves cisterns, broken cisterns that can hold no water."[6] Again, eternal life is found on the inside. As David said, we know Him "in the innermost being...in the hidden part"—not out in the world but in the hidden part inside us. John wrote, "For all that is in the world, the lust of the flesh and the lust of the eyes and the boastful pride of life, is not from the Father, but is from the world."[7]

Paul said in the Book of Colossians that the mystery of the gospel is Christ *in you*.[8] All the treasures of wisdom and knowledge are in Christ, and where is Christ? *In you.* Jesus said He would become *within us* a well of living water springing up to eternal life so we would thirst no more.[9]

Authentic prayer happens when we connect with God in the hidden part of our nature, our innermost being. This is one reason Jesus speaks about going into a prayer closet, a secret place, when we pray.[10] But there's a price to pay for this. Many of us experience an excruciating pain when we disconnect from the outer world to sit before the Lord to connect with Him in our innermost being. We feel a type of anxiety when we put down our smartphones. It's like we're going through withdrawal when we're not being stimulated by the things of the world that we use to satisfy ourselves, trying to fill the void in our souls.

But if we're willing to die to ourselves and fast from those things from the outer world that are connected to the flesh, then we will slowly discover God on the inside. The reward of going through this process is that we'll be able to drink of the well of eternal life that's found not on the outside but on the inside of man, where the Lord has placed His Son and Spirit. Yeshua said, "He who believes in Me, as the Scripture said, 'From his innermost being will flow rivers of living water.'"[11]

Eternity is found within. Solomon wrote in Ecclesiastes that God has placed eternity in our hearts.[12] Paul prayed that "the eyes of your understanding [would be] enlightened; that you may know what is the hope of His calling, what are the riches of the glory of His inheritance *in the* saints."[13] This verse tells us that God's inheritance is in the saints. It's not in the world, not in something you can see on the outside; it's invisible—it's on the inside. This is where our connection with the Lord is.

The Power of Fasting

I said previously that getting in touch with this place that David called the innermost being involves fasting. I say this because fasting helps us disconnect from the things the outer man is connected to. Fasting involves cutting ourselves off from everything in the material, visible world that we look to for satisfaction. Jesus said, "Whoever loses his life for My sake will find it."[14] There's a price to pay to get in touch with your inner man: a dying to the flesh.

Jesus said, "If anyone wishes to come after Me, he must deny himself, and take up his cross and follow Me."[15] We must come to a place of radical obedience in denying the flesh to become connected to Father God and be fused with His Spirit inside us. As long as we're looking to and running after things outside ourselves for satisfaction, we'll never find God in a deeper way.

When we connect with God in our innermost being, wisdom encases us. David said, "In the hidden part You will make me know wisdom."[16] In Judaism, wisdom is the chief attribute of God. For example, in the Book of Proverbs, God is speaking to us as *wisdom personified*.

Wisdom shouts in the street, she lifts her voice in the square; at the head of the noisy streets she cries out; at the entrance of the gates in the city she utters her sayings: "How long, O naive ones, will you love being simple-minded? And scoffers delight themselves in scoffing and fools hate knowledge? Turn to my reproof, behold, I will pour out my spirit on you; I will make my words known to you."[17]

Wisdom is the ability to understand, but wisdom is more than that. Wisdom is the most primordial way of knowing God. It's an understanding at a deeper level than objective fact; it's a knowing. This is what God wants to do in us. He wants to bring us into a place of knowing Him.

But again, there's a price to pay. A holy and godly discipline is required to get to this place where you become aware of what's going on inside you, because we are born into this world connected to the outer world. Jesus said, "That which is born of the flesh is flesh, and that which is born of the Spirit is spirit. Do not be amazed that I said to you, 'You must be born again.'"[18]

When you're born into the world through your mother's womb, you're born flesh. Flesh is connected to our senses, which connect us to the outer world—to what we see, the food we depend on, the air we breathe, our physical and sexual passions, and so on.

In order to get connected to the Spirit who dwells in us, we have to separate ourselves from the flesh, and this takes a godly discipline. This is why Paul said, "Discipline yourself for the purpose of godliness; for bodily discipline is only of little profit, but godliness is profitable for all things, since it holds promise for the present life and also for the life to come."[19]

I'm not someone who has fully arrived. I'm on the journey, just as we all are on the road to perfection. Paul said of himself: "Not that I have already obtained it or have already become perfect, but I press on so that I may lay hold of that for which also I was laid hold of by Christ Jesus....I press on toward the goal for the prize of the upward call of God in Christ Jesus."[20]

We are all on a journey, but there are practical steps we can take to connect with the Spirit of God. Here are a few:

1. Get up earlier to start your day alone with God in worship, the Word, and prayer. Whether it's the first fifteen minutes or the first hour, do something to give the Lord the first part of your day.

2. Be self-aware so you control your tongue and only speak words that give life. Don't let words of criticism, hatred, accusation, negativity, or complaining come out of your mouth. Be conscious of your speech and discipline your tongue.

> For we all stumble in many ways. If anyone does not stumble in what he says, he is a perfect man, able to bridle the whole body as well. Now if we put the bits into the horses' mouths so that they will obey us, we direct their entire body as well. Look at the ships also, though they are so great and are driven by strong winds, are still directed

by a very small rudder wherever the inclination of the pilot desires. So also the tongue is a small part of the body, and yet it boasts of great things.

See how great a forest is set aflame by such a small fire! And the tongue is a fire, the very world of iniquity; the tongue is set among our members as that which defiles the entire body, and sets on fire the course of our life, and is set on fire by hell. For every species of beasts and birds, of reptiles and creatures of the sea, is tamed and has been tamed by the human race. But no one can tame the tongue; it is a restless evil and full of deadly poison. With it we bless our Lord and Father, and with it we curse men, who have been made in the likeness of God; from the same mouth come both blessing and cursing. My brethren, these things ought not to be this way.[21]

Yeshua said, "It is not what enters into the mouth that defiles the man, but what proceeds out of the mouth, this defiles the man."

3. Don't watch television shows or videos that would displease the Lord. Whether you're watching on TV or on YouTube, Instagram, TikTok, Snapchat, or any other social media, avoid programs that you know the Lord would be unhappy with you watching or that do not edify you in growing in your relationship with HaShem. I try not to watch or listen to anything that isn't moving me forward in building my relationship with God. I don't want to be legalistic, but these are just commonsense, godly disciplines if we're really serious about knowing Him.

Paul had a vision of what was possible, and he was pursuing it with his whole life. And as he pursued it, he was entering more and more into the fullness of it. It's the same for you and me; we're pressing "on toward the goal for the prize of the upward call of God in Christ Jesus."

A Deeper Cleansing

As he continues in prayer, David realizes that in order to enter into this reality, this fullness, he needs a deeper cleansing. He prays, "Purify me with hyssop, and I shall be clean; wash me, and I shall be whiter than snow. Make me to hear joy and gladness, let the bones which You have broken rejoice."[22]

This verse reminds me of a dream I had several years ago. In the dream, my wife and I were traveling and stopped to stay the night at the home of my former martial arts instructor. When we arrived, he took us upstairs to show us where we would be staying—and promptly guided us into the bathroom. (If you think that's weird, you haven't heard anything yet!) Suddenly he jumped into the toilet bowl and was shrunk down inside a translucent egg. I could see him inside the egg, surrounded by blue sanitizing fluid, and yet he was joyful, content, and safe. A few seconds later he was standing beside us again, back in full stature and acting as if everything were normal.

The dream continued with my wife and me making our bed the following morning and going downstairs to tell my former instructor that we were leaving. To our surprise he stopped us in our tracks. "Wait a second," he said. "Before you leave, let's take a look at the room and make sure it's clean."

I was taken aback, but we went upstairs, and he began inspecting the room. I knew we had made the bed and cleaned up. In addition, we had stayed for only one night; how much mess could we have made?

I was stunned, then, when my martial arts instructor pulled the dresser in the room away from the wall, took out a toothbrush, and began scrubbing the wall by the baseboard behind the dresser. "You're not ready to leave yet," he said. "You haven't scrubbed back here yet."

I was scratching my head, thinking, "All we did was sleep in his room for one night. Does he think we got it dirty back behind the dresser by the baseboard?"

He then reached behind the dresser, pulled out something that looked like an electrical box, and told me to reset it.

I had never seen anything like this. It was attached to the wall by what looked like telephone wire and appeared to have only a single button on top. So I reset it by doing the only thing I knew to do: push the button.

As I did, he said, "No, you're not doing it right. You're not thinking." And with that he got down on his knees, grabbed the gadget, and flipped open a side panel that I had not seen. Suddenly I could see that this gadget had many buttons inside. He entered a combination and reset the device, and then the dream ended.

I awoke with a strong sense that this dream, despite

being strange, was directly from God. When I asked Him to reveal its meaning, I sensed Him saying, "You are on a journey. But before you can continue on this journey, we need to clean up the filth in your heart and in your life. I am sanitizing you from the scum you picked up living in this world, through your own sin, and through generational curses. I'm cleansing you of that filth so you are able to move on."

He then explained the second part of my dream, involving cleaning behind the dresser. The Lord was telling me, "I want to go deeper. You think you're clean because you've taken care of a lot of issues in your life. To your credit, you have tried to clean as much as you could. But I want to go much deeper. I want to cleanse you from deep within your heart."

"But what about the electrical box thing? What was that?" I asked.

"I want to reset your thinking," He explained. "But to reset it, I need you to begin thinking about what you are thinking. You assumed one thing about the box because that's all you could see, but you weren't thinking the way I want you to. I need to reset the way you process things so you can capture every thought. I want to reprogram your mind so you can move forward in your journey."

I share that dream because I believe God is saying to you and me that He wants to cleanse us so we can move into a deeper place of fellowship with Him. He wants us to allow Him to show us the places deep in our hearts that we need Him to purify. He's calling us to examine our thoughts and allow Him to cleanse and reprogram our minds.

In the dream, my martial arts instructor was joyful when he was in the blue sanitizing fluid. I believe the Lord was revealing to me the same thing He showed David—that as we allow Father God to cleanse us, we'll have joy.

David asked to be washed and purified, and then he prayed, "Make me to hear joy and gladness, let the bones which You have broken rejoice."[23] David understood that we can't have joy without first being cleansed. But how many people are in churches trying to have joy without ever having been washed? They're living in spiritual mediocrity. They want to rejoice and celebrate, but they can only do it as long as the worship music is playing at a decibel that's making everybody lose their hearing. They think that's joy, but that's not joy. They're just being pumped up by the bassline or the drumbeat. Real joy is not dependent on the volume of the music or percussion in the sanctuary. True joy exists in the inner man, and it is connected to being clean on the inside. David prayed for joy, but he realized he couldn't have true, lasting joy until he was first washed.

David went on to say, "Create in me a clean heart, O God, and renew a steadfast spirit within me."[24] He knew he couldn't fix himself, and neither can you and I. But we can be encouraged by the fact that the Lord will complete what He started in us. The apostle Paul wrote, "I am confident of this very thing, that He who began a good work in you will perfect it until the day of Christ Jesus."[25] So while we are endeavoring to overcome every day in practical ways, we can also know that God is working within us by His Spirit, changing and transforming us. "Not by works of righteousness which we have done, but according to His mercy He saved us, through the washing of regeneration and renewing of the Holy Spirit."[26] This process of transformation is a partnership between God and man.

As we close this chapter, I want to encourage you to remember that prayer does not have to be audible. Prayer can simply be the cry of your heart. Whether it's silently in your soul or your thoughts or out loud, prayer is your reaching out to God. And authentic prayer involves asking God to wash and cleanse you. It involves the purification of your inner being. I oftentimes pray David's words in Psalm 19: "Let the words of my mouth and the meditation of my heart be acceptable in Your sight, O Lord."[27]

Beloved one, not only are we dealing with the world, the flesh, and the devil; we're also dealing with ourselves and what Paul described as the evil inclination in our own souls.[28] Every day, we are in a battle. We have to overcome evil and our flesh. This is why Jesus said, "To him who overcomes, I will grant to eat of the tree of life which is in the Paradise of God."[29]

Jesus the Messiah is always watching you and me, and He said, "Behold, I am coming quickly, and My reward is with Me, to render to every man according to what he has done."[30]

Let's be ready!

Chapter 4

THE REALITY OF CHRIST IN YOU

WHEN YOU TRULY connect with God in your inner man, you realize that you don't have to jump through hoops to enter God's presence. When I was a young believer, I used to think I always had to get on my knees to pray. At times while I was lying in my bed, I would be inspired by the Holy Spirit with what I call awakenings. These were like sudden impulses of light, and whenever one would hit me, I would feel the need to get out of bed and kneel at the foot of my bed to pray for whatever it was that struck me. I did this hundreds of times for years, and that was fine. It was part of my journey and process of growth. But eventually the Holy Spirit began to show me I didn't have to get out of bed and get on my knees to pray every time He spoke to me. I sensed Him telling me I was already kneeling before Him in my heart.

God wants us to know that we don't have to do something on the outside in the physical world to get Him to hear us. When our hearts are in fellowship with Him, that is enough. This is important for us to understand. It's important that we become so centered in the Holy Spirit that we know God isn't necessarily requiring us to do something on the outside to connect with Him. The communion is already happening within, and we just need to trust Him that whatever we're desiring from Him is already done.

Yeshua said, "Therefore I say to you, all things for which you pray and ask, believe that you have received them, and they will be *granted* you."[1] Now, I realize that sometimes we need to keep asking and contending to enter more and more into our inheritance and God's fullness. But sometimes the way forward is to believe we have already received it and that it is already done.

In Ephesians 3, Paul prayed "that He would grant you, according to the riches of His glory, to be strengthened with power through His Spirit in the inner man, so that Christ may dwell in your hearts through faith."[2] God wants us to know that He hears the slightest whisper, the slightest inclination of our hearts because He's connected to our inner man. This is why you don't have to get out of bed and kneel in order for God to hear or answer your prayer. What God desires is for you to simply believe that He heard you and that He will answer.

This is where real intimacy comes from—when you get to the place where you don't think you have to do something externally to connect with God, but know that the Ruach HaKodesh is in you and nothing outside yourself is required. "In Him you have been made complete."[3]

Eventually, the Lord showed me something during that time when I felt like I always had to do something for Him to hear me, when I'd have the inspiration inside to pray about something and I'd think, "Oh, I have to get on my knees and pray." I started noticing that as soon as I got to the foot of my bed to get on my knees, I no longer sensed the connection.

I sensed the connection and felt inspired when I first

experienced the inclination to connect with God, but when I did something outside of myself—got out of bed to get on my knees—the connection was lost. I was trying to receive more by getting out of my bed, thinking God would answer me if I did that. But when I reached the foot of my bed and got on my knees, I didn't feel that same connection anymore. Why? Because I went from trying to connect with God from my inside to doing something on the outside, and I lost the connection as a result.

In his prayer in Ephesians 3, Paul is saying, "I'm asking the Lord to strengthen you by His power, so you will know that He dwells inside you, and by coming into that revelation, you'll enter into deep communion with Him." Let me say it again: You don't have to reach outside yourself to connect with God. The Holy Spirit is in you now. Jesus said the kingdom of heaven is not here or there "for, behold, the kingdom of God is within you."⁴ This is the mystery of the gospel. This is the mystery of having fellowship with God.

Again, the apostle Paul wrote:

> Of this church I was made a minister according to the stewardship from God bestowed on me for your benefit, so that I might fully carry out the preaching of the word of God, that is, the mystery which has been hidden from the past ages and generations, but has now been manifested to His saints, to whom God willed to make known what is the riches of the glory of this mystery among

the Gentiles, which is *Christ in you, the hope of glory.*[5]

This is deep calling to deep. Connecting with God through prayer on the inside is a supernatural river to answered prayer, and it's the pathway to discovering how close to you God is. When you discover God inside you and begin to fellowship with Him in that place, you will enter a whole new level of eternal life.

Strengthened in the Inner Man

Many people have a real relationship with Jesus, but they're praying to a Jesus who is out "there" somewhere. They're praying to a Jesus who's up in heaven. They're praying to someone who is outside themselves. But notice that Paul's prayer is that we would come to the realization that Christ is not first out there somewhere, although He is at the Father's right hand, but that He is in our inner man:

> For this reason I bow my knees before the Father…
> that He would grant you, according to the riches of
> His glory, to be strengthened with power through
> His Spirit in the inner man, so that Christ may
> dwell in your hearts through faith.[6]

When we're strengthened by the Spirit with the Father's power, we enter into an experiential reality in which we comprehend that God is inside us through Yeshua by the Holy Spirit. Until we receive and experience this revelation, we'll never feel intimately connected to our Father. The only way to apprehend this reality is by being strengthened on the inside by God's power through His Spirit.

Paul continues by saying that this strengthening in our inner man creates a place for Christ to be at rest and make His home in us: "so that Christ may dwell in your hearts through faith."[7] Now, when we think of this word *faith* that Paul uses, a lot of times we think of some type of outward projection—faith that moves mountains or faith that brings healing. This is true of faith's results. But faith is the result of revelation. When we're strengthened by God's Spirit, we are able to apprehend by revelation, which produces the faith.

Consider with me a passage from Matthew 16.

> Now when Jesus came into the district of Caesarea Philippi, He was asking His disciples, "Who do people say that the Son of Man is?" And they said, "Some say John the Baptist; and others, Elijah; but still others, Jeremiah, or one of the prophets." He said to them, "But who do you say that I am?" Simon Peter answered, "You are the Christ, the Son of the living God." And Jesus said to him, "Blessed are you, Simon Barjona, because flesh and blood did not reveal this to you, but My Father who is in heaven. I also say to you that you are Peter, and upon this rock I will build My church; and the gates of Hades will not overpower it."[8]

This is one of the best-known, most important, and hotly debated portions of Scripture in theological circles.

Christian institutions of higher learning have very different and conflicting understandings of what this passage means. Catholics believe the "rock" that Jesus speaks of here refers to Peter, whom Catholics believe was their first pope. Thus, the traditional Catholic interpretation of this passage is that the church is built on the rock of the papacy. They would say that to this very day, every Catholic pope, beginning with Peter, is the rock upon which the church is being built.

Protestants teach that the "rock" Jesus is referring to in this passage is Peter's confession of faith, "You are the Christ."[9] In other words, Protestants believe the church is built upon our belief and confession that Jesus is the Christ, the Anointed One. While this is certainly true, I believe there is something even deeper going on here.

Notice Yeshua's response after Peter made his faith declaration that Jesus is the Christ: "Blessed are you, Simon Barjona, because flesh and blood did not reveal this to you, but My Father who is in heaven. I also say to you that you are Peter, and upon this rock I will build My church; and the gates of Hades will not overpower it."[10] I believe the rock that Jesus built His church on is revelation. Yeshua said, "You're blessed, Peter, because you don't know who I am on your own. My Father *revealed* it to you, and on *this rock* I will build My church." When we receive revelation, solid-rock faith is produced. This is why Messiah said, "Everyone who has heard and learned from the Father comes to Me."[11]

As we apprehend by revelation that Jesus is in us, a fellowship develops, a deliverance from loneliness, a deep security that is rooted in our inner man. We know we don't have to go to heaven or to the bottom of the sea to apprehend God because He's inside us. When we grasp this, an intimacy, a divine synergy takes place that causes us to begin to walk in a love relationship with God that produces a deep security in our souls. Jesus said He is "meek and lowly in heart."[12] He was so secure in the Father's love that He didn't have to broadcast Himself, and this produced a meekness and a lowliness of heart.

The focal point of our prayer is to know Him and enter into eternal life. Many think that eternal life is just about going to heaven when we die. But eternal life is also now. Eternity is beyond time. Jesus Himself is the eternal One. This same truth is revealed in Martha's conversation with Jesus after her brother Lazarus had died.

> Martha then said to Jesus, "Lord, if You had been here, my brother would not have died. Even now I know that whatever You ask of God, God will give You." Jesus said to her, "Your brother will rise again." Martha said to Him, "I know that he will rise again in the resurrection on the last day." Jesus said to her, "I am the resurrection and the life; he who believes in Me will live even if he dies, and everyone who lives and believes in Me will never die. Do you believe this?"[13]

To the degree that we have entered into fellowship with God, the eternal One, we are living in the realm of eternity.

Rooted in Love

Yeshua said when we abide in Him, our prayers will be answered: "If you abide in Me, and My words abide in you, ask whatever you wish, and it will be done for you."[14] How do we abide in Yeshua? By living out of His love.

> This is My commandment, that you love one another, just as I have loved you....You did not choose Me but I chose you, and appointed you that you would go and bear fruit, and that your fruit would remain, so that whatever you ask of the Father in My name He may give to you. This I command you, that you love one another.[15]

Paul tells us in Ephesians 3:17 that apprehending the Father in our inner man will result in us "being rooted and grounded in love." We're not just being loving people; we're rooted in God's love. A lot of times people think because one of the fruit of the Spirit is love, they should go around being do-gooders. It's true that we should do good, but that's not where love starts. It starts with being rooted in knowing God's love for you. That's what Paul is talking about—that you would be rooted and grounded in the love of God and "able to comprehend with all the saints what is the breadth and length and height and depth" of His love for you.[16]

The Father's love is more enormous and infinite than the sky. It's deeper than the deepest ocean and surpasses the height, depth, breadth, and width of anything we can understand. There are no words to describe the depth and power of God's love. It's so big and wide, my words are admittedly empty in trying to describe it.

Paul is doing his best to convey how super-colossal the ocean of God's love is. He wants us "to know the love of Christ *which surpasses knowledge*."[17]

Think about this: all the Father's love is directed to His Son. John 1:18 says the Son is "in the bosom of the Father."

The Father is love, and love by its very nature needs to be focused on someone. Through all eternity, God the Father loved His Son, who has always been inside Him. All the strength of the Father's love is focused on Jesus. Now receive this: you have been grafted into Jesus. So the same love the Father directs toward His only begotten Son, Jesus, is now focused just as passionately on you and me because we are in Christ. This is what Paul is praying that we would comprehend—"what is the breadth and length and height and depth, and to know the love of Christ which surpasses knowledge, that you may be filled up to all the fullness of God."[18]

As I shared in an earlier chapter, everyone is searching to be filled up with something. We are creatures of desire. Human nature is that we need to be filled. God created us to be filled with Himself, but unfortunately, in our deception we seek to fill the void within us with things that can't satisfy. This is why the Lord said in the Book of Jeremiah, "My people...have forsaken Me, the fountain of living waters, to hew for themselves cisterns, broken cisterns that can hold no water."[19] Of course, He was speaking of Himself as the fountain of living water. He was saying in essence, "Why do you seek to draw water from cisterns that hold no water? Why are you trying to drink from something that will not satisfy you?"

What the Lord is promising in Ephesians 3 is that as we come to comprehend His love for us, we're going to be filled up with the fullness of God. The things in life that really matter are things that cannot be seen. When it's time to leave this world, will it really matter how white our teeth are? Are we really going to care about the car we drove? Are we really going to be concerned about our house? Is the job we had really going to be important? No. The things that really matter are the intangibles—the relationships we've built. When people are on their deathbed, they don't regret not buying a different car. They regret not spending more time with their loved ones, asking for forgiveness, and reaching out to people or helping others. This shows us again that the things that really satisfy the human soul are not based in the material world but in love. This is what the Father is calling us to—to enter into this comprehension of His love for us so we can be filled up with *the fullness of God.*

So as we return to the theme of prayer, consider

this: Paul ends his prayer in Ephesians 3 by saying that the One who raised Jesus from the dead "is able to do exceedingly abundantly above all that we ask or think."[20] Whatever you're believing God for, whatever you'd like to see the Father do for you, let me tell you, Father God has something even better in store than what you are asking for. "Eye has not seen, nor ear heard, nor have entered into the heart of man the things which God has prepared for those who love Him."[21]

Chapter 5

BREAK THROUGH INTO ETERNITY

W E SHOULD TALK to God about everything, but if we really have the mindset God wants for us, our greatest prayer is going to be to know Him. Jesus said to as many as believed Him, He gave the gift of eternal life.[1] But what is eternal life? Jesus said in the Gospel of John, "This is eternal life, *that they may know You*, the only true God, and Jesus Christ whom You have sent."[2] Prayer is all about breakthrough into eternity. It is about entering into a state of knowing God in our deepest *kishkes*—in the depths of our insides.

When we know the Lord and begin to commune with Him deep in our hearts, we will find ourselves being concerned with what He wants for us rather than what we want for ourselves. This too is part of genuine prayer. Authentic prayer is about desiring the things God desires for us. It's not simply coming to Him asking for the things we think we need. These "needs" are often just temporary, fleshly desires from the world that we think are going to bring fulfillment. But as we have seen in previous chapters, true satisfaction is found in knowing Jesus. Yeshua said, "I came that they may have life, and have it abundantly,"[3] and, "If the Son makes you free, you will be free indeed."[4]

Consider also Yeshua's conversation with the woman at the well after He asked her for a drink.

> Therefore the Samaritan woman said to Him, "How is it that You, being a Jew, ask me for a drink since I am a Samaritan woman?" (For Jews have

no dealings with Samaritans.) Jesus answered and said to her, "If you knew the gift of God, and who it is who says to you, 'Give Me a drink,' you would have asked Him, and He would have given you living water."

She said to Him, "Sir, You have nothing to draw with and the well is deep; where then do You get that living water? You are not greater than our father Jacob, are You, who gave us the well, and drank of it himself and his sons and his cattle?" Jesus answered and said to her, "Everyone who drinks of this water will thirst again; but whoever drinks of the water that I will give him shall never thirst; but the water that I will give him will become in him a well of water springing up to eternal life."[5]

In His encounter with the woman, Jesus was telling us that if we would yield to Him and submit to His mastery in our lives, His Spirit within us would become like a well of living water springing up to eternal life so we would hunger and thirst no more.

The challenge for many who are naming the name of Jesus is that they're looking for this abundant life, this satisfaction that Jesus spoke of, by simply asking God to add to their lives the things of the world. But as I stated previously, the Bible says, "All that is in the world, the lust of the flesh and the lust of the eyes and the boastful pride of life, is not from the Father, but is from the world."[6]

We see things and say, "Oh, I want this, and I want

that." But Scripture teaches that all these things that we think we want cannot truly satisfy us. Authentic prayer happens when we transition from just asking the Father for the things we want from the world to instead saying: "Father, I want the deeper things. I want to enter into a reality that the world can't take away. I want to lay hold of You so that when I get old and my hairs are gray, my leaf will not wither.[7] I want to have joy even in my old age because my joy won't be dependent on the world or my status in the world. It will be dependent on the relationship I have forged with You and on connecting with You in a deeper way."

What God has for you and me is on a totally different level. It comes from way down deep. It comes from knowing the Father and the security of being in relationship with Him. It comes from knowing who you are to Him, that you're loved, blessed, and secure, and that because of who you are, your future is bright—very bright.

Please meditate with me on a profound section of God's Word that many have not thoroughly considered. It is John 13:3–4:

> Jesus, knowing that the Father had given all things into His hands, and that He had come forth from God and was going back to God, got up from supper, and laid aside His garments; and taking a towel, He girded Himself.

What's going on here? There are three important points I want to make about this passage.

First, Yeshua knew He was completely blessed. He knew "that the Father had given all things into His hands." We need to pray for the revelation of what we have! Paul said in Ephesians 1:3, "Blessed be the God and Father of our Lord Jesus Christ, who has blessed us with every spiritual blessing in the heavenly places in Christ." Yeshua knew He was blessed with the fullness of the Father's blessing. We need to pray for the comprehension of the blessing that rests upon our lives. Paul prayed "that you will know...what are the riches of the glory of His inheritance in the saints."[8] In other words, Paul prayed that we would know what we have.

We need to be asking and contending for revelation of what is already ours. For example, Yeshua said, "My peace I give to you."[9] If you think about it, isn't this what humanity prays for, to have peace and rest and to be whole? Jesus said He has given that to us. Notice also that Yeshua said He gave us His joy: "These things I have spoken to you so that My joy may be in you, and that your joy may be made full."[10]

Several years ago I became really frustrated with God. I was saying to Him, "Father, I've been praying for Your peace, for Your joy, and for Your freedom all these years. Where is it?" I was really desperate, and the Holy Spirit instructed me, "You've already got it. You need to claim that it's in you and that I've already given it to you." It's the same with the mind of Christ. We're all looking for soundness of mind, but the Bible tells us we have the mind of Christ.[11]

Everything we're looking for is ours in Christ, and we need to take hold of the fact that we already possess these things. It is a dual reality. We possess these eternal realities that we need to claim, yet at the same time we contend to enter more fully into the experience of these blessings.

What I want to emphasize here is that fulfillment will not come from anything on the outside. It will come in Christ, and it will come from the inside. We need to stop asking for Father to bless us with the things of the world and start asking Him instead for revelation and comprehension of what we already have in Him. Yeshua was free, first of all, because He knew "that the Father had given all things into His hands."[12] We likewise have already been blessed "with every spiritual blessing in the heavenly places."[13] Affirm it, claim it, and declare it.

Second, Yeshua understood His identity. We escape the delusion of looking to and asking for the things of the world to satisfy us when we find our identity in God. Notice what we read in John 13:3: Yeshua knew "that He had come forth from God." In other words, beloved one, He knew who He was. It doesn't matter how big of a house we have, what car we drive, what our position is at the workplace, and so on. If we don't have a positive identity, we will never be satisfied. Our self-identity is at the core of our potential for happiness and fulfillment.

Yeshua knew who He was. He knew He was the best. He was the Son of the great I Am, and He knew He was loved. When you know who your Daddy is, when your Daddy is God and you know you're His child, you know you're the best. Give us full revelation of this, I pray, Father.

Remember with me what happened at Yeshua's baptism.

> Now when all the people were baptized, Jesus was also baptized, and while He was praying, heaven was opened, and the Holy Spirit descended upon Him in bodily form like a dove, and a voice came out of heaven, "You are My beloved Son, in You I am well-pleased."[14]

Consider that this was the foundational launching point of Yeshua's ministry. Those present heard the Father's words of affirmation over His Son.[15] I want you to focus on the fact that at the center of everything Yeshua did was the awareness that He was the Father's beloved Son. This is why Yeshua was satisfied, content, and whole. He was not looking to the world to fulfill His longings. He was fulfilled by His Father:

> Meanwhile the disciples were urging Him, saying, "Rabbi, eat." But He said to them, "I have food to eat that you do not know about." So the disciples were saying to one another, "No one brought Him anything to eat, did he?"[16]

Rather than focusing on our temporal needs in prayer, we ought to be asking Father to help us know who we are to Him. We need to press in, contending to receive our identity from the Father. Yeshua knew who He was to the Father and in the Father. This is why He is self-fulfilled and has abundant life.

Finally, Yeshua knew His future was secure. Notice that John 13:3 says Yeshua knew He "was going back to God."[17] In other words, He knew His future was both secure and glorious. He knew there was no battle that could sink Him. He knew nothing in His future was going to conquer Him. He wasn't afraid of what lay ahead. He wasn't afraid of death. He wasn't afraid of sickness. He wasn't afraid of going broke. He wasn't afraid of somebody deserting Him. He wasn't afraid of anything because He knew He was going back to God.

What about you and me? Do we really believe our future is secure and glorious, or do we spend our lives worrying about and fearing what is going to happen tomorrow, next month, or next year? More of the world's goods will not make us happy. But being convinced and secure that our future is bright and protected will. Peter wrote that we are destined "to obtain an inheritance which is imperishable and undefiled and will not fade away, reserved in heaven for [us], who are protected by the power of God through faith for a salvation ready to be revealed in the last time."[18] This is why Yeshua said to His disciples, "Rejoice that your names are recorded in heaven."[19]

Let's every day rejoice, praise God, and thank Yeshua that we're going to heaven!

These things I have written to you who believe in the name of the Son of God, so that you may know that you have eternal life.[20]

Yes, life can get pretty difficult at times, but isn't it tremendous to know that "God causes all things to work together for good" in our lives.[21]

Beloved one, I hope to convince you that more of the world is not what we need. What we need is a greater revelation of what we have and who we are in Him. This is where our prayer focus should be.

Therefore if you have been raised up with Christ, keep seeking the things above, where Christ is, seated at the right hand of God. Set your mind on the things above, not on the things that are on earth. For you have died and your life is hidden with Christ in God.[22]

Notice that phrase "your life is hidden with Christ in God." What does this mean? We exist, live by, and draw from an invisible Spirit. Our power, joy, strength, soundness of mind, and fullness, along with every other quality of what is true life, are being administered to us from a God who cannot be seen by the world or by the naked eye.

So let's not put our primary focus on the visible things of the world, but instead, let's take Yeshua's words fully to heart: "Seek first His kingdom and His righteousness and all these things [all the world has to offer] will be added to you."[23]

CONFORMED TO JESUS' IMAGE

The goal of our prayer should, first of all, be that we would know God, and then that in knowing Him we would be conformed to the image of His Son: "for those whom He foreknew, He also predestined to become conformed to the image of His Son, so that He would be the firstborn among many brethren."[24]

The Son existed for the Father: "My food is to do the will of Him who sent Me and to accomplish His work."[25] If we want to move into the deep places in our prayer experience, we need to be asking, "Father, what do You want from me? What's Your desire for my life? Where do You want to connect with me? What do I need to forsake? What do I need to let go of? How can I enter into a deeper place with You so I can fulfill Your purpose for my life?"

When Jesus taught us to pray, He began and ended the Lord's Prayer in the same way—by focusing on the Father's will. He said, "Pray, then, in this way: 'Our Father who is in heaven, hallowed be Your name. Your kingdom come. Your will be done, on earth as it is in heaven."[26] Then He ended it with: "For Yours is the kingdom and the power and the glory forever. Amen." He was focused on the Father, the holiness of God, and being pleasing to Him. He wasn't looking to the Father to first meet His personal needs. He was primarily concerned about the Father being glorified. This is the heartbeat that should propel our prayers also.

Beloved one, if we want to see God move in our lives, if

we want to witness Him answering our prayers, we have to ask Him for the right things. John wrote in one of his letters, "This is the confidence which we have before Him, that, *if we ask anything according to His will,* He hears us. And if we know that He hears us in whatever we ask, we know that we have the requests which we have asked from Him."[27] No matter how much fleshly faith we think we have, if we are not praying according to God's will for our lives, our requests will bear little fruit. If the things we're asking Him for are the same things Father wants for us, we can know our prayers are going to give us breakthrough.

Some people might think it's not very exciting to pray God's will. They think what God wants for them is boring. For instance, some people think heaven is going to be a place where angels float around with harps all day and people sit with nothing to do. They're not excited about heaven because they have a wrong concept of what it is. In the same way, some think that God's will is boring. They think living a Christian life means being a goody two-shoes and they will not have fun. What a delusion! I love David's words in Psalm 16:11, "In Your presence is fullness of joy; in Your right hand there are pleasures forever." Doing God's will made David Israel's greatest king and a very, very powerful man.

I recently wrote a book called *The Key to Answered Prayer* that is focused on praying the types of prayers modeled by the apostles and prophets of the Bible. It is a burden in my heart to encourage people to pray God's will for their lives because when we do, our prayers will be answered and we will slowly enter into the freedom and abundant life that Messiah promised.

A MASSIVE SHIFT

I had an experience several years ago related to praying God's will that brought a critical shift in my ministry. I was leading a series of outdoor meetings, and many people were attending every night. I was preaching the gospel, and at the end of my message, I would invite people to come to the altar for prayer. I would go one by one to each person who came forward and ask, "What moved you to come forward today? What are you looking to God to do for you?" Oftentimes they would say, "Pray for me that I will get a different job," or, "Pray for me that I will get my credit card spending under control," or, "Pray for me that I will find a spouse," or, "Pray for me that I'll be able to have a baby."

All these requests are important, and I don't want to minimize any of them at all. But as I was praying for people night after night, the Holy Spirit subtly spoke to my heart and said, "I don't want you to just pray for people according to what they're asking you to pray for them about. I want you to look to Me about what to pray for them."

A massive shift took place. I no longer just prayed for people according to their requests. I didn't dismiss what they asked me to pray for, but I would ask, "Lord, what do You want me to pray for them about?" Sometimes they'd ask me to be in agreement with them about receiving some type of earthly blessing, but the Holy Spirit would cause me to know that there was sin in their lives and they were knowingly in disobedience to God. The Lord would tell me, "That's what I want you to pray. I want you to pray for them to repent." Sometimes the Lord would even give me a specific word about what they needed to repent of.

When I began to seek God's will for them and not just pray what they wanted, a real empowerment came over my ministry. This gets to the heart of this principle of prayer—when we're praying according to God's will, God is going to move, and we can be confident He is going to answer.

When I am in Africa, for example, so many people ask me to pray for them, and I usually pray something like this: "Father, I pray that You would give my friend the same love for You that Jesus has. Father, I pray that You would burn into his heart the same passionate love for You that Your Son has for You, that You would set his heart ablaze with Jesus' love for You." Now, this person might have come to me and said, "Rabbi, will you pray that God will bless my business?" That's important. But because this individual may not be dedicated to the Lord in his personal life, rather than just launching into a prayer for God to bless his business, I would say, "Father, I pray that You'll circumcise so-and-so's heart with divine fire and put within him the love for You that Jesus has." That's the type of prayer, beloved one, that God is going to answer.

We may think our need is financial or healing in our

relationships, but having Jesus' love for the Father in our heart answers every question. So often the things we think we need are not really what we need. And more important, they're not going to satisfy us. The things we find ourselves praying for oftentimes are the lust of the eyes, the lust of the flesh, and the boastful pride of life. The devil used these same pseudo realities to tempt Eve away from God in the Garden. He put the fruit in front of her, and it appealed to her flesh. She thought it would taste good and make her feel good and feel important.

She ate of the fruit, not realizing she wasn't really lacking anything to begin with because she had Father God. Then she gave the fruit to her husband, Adam, and he ate of it, and the powers of darkness entered the world. Ever since then, mankind has been chasing after the lust of the eyes, the lust of the flesh, and prestige in the world's eyes, and many people's prayer lives show they are still being controlled by these desires.

A lot of preachers are promising people that they can get everything they want in this world. They tell us, "This is how you can have a promotion," or, "This is how you can have more money." Those teachings are not really focusing on the primary message of God's heart. God's will for us is deeper than what we see in the material world, and the things God wants for us will truly satisfy. This is why the lives of so many people who have what everyone thinks they should want are in shambles. They're depressed, divorced, addicted to drugs or alcohol, and even suicidal.

Beloved one, I think we agree that the things the

world offers can't really satisfy, so let's not focus on just asking God for surface things. Let's go deeper and focus our prayer lives on asking God for that which is according to His will.

Jesus lived His life seeking the Father's will. When He was praying in the Garden of Gethsemane, knowing the time was near for Him to shed His blood on the cross, Yeshua prayed, "Father, if You are willing, remove this cup from Me; yet not My will, but Yours be done."[28] When we make God's will the priority of our prayer lives, we'll receive an empowerment by God's Spirit. I love 2 Chronicles 27:6, "So Jotham became mighty because he ordered his ways before the Lord his God." When we seek God's will, we will be led to a place where we're living in victory and experiencing divine satisfaction. The Holy Spirit will then fill up our souls, and we'll enter into a communion with God in the Spirit—a sense that we're in Him and He's in us—that truly satisfies our souls.

Beloved one, these are the ends our prayer lives need to be driven toward—not more of this or that but more of Him.

Chapter 6

SUPERNATURAL UNITY WITH GOD

IN MY QUEST to know God and enter into authentic communion with Him, what I desire most is to become one with Him. I want to know Jesus in me and around me and experience His power. I want to be transformed into the likeness of Yeshua and be empowered by His Spirit to ascend through the darkness and walk in supernatural victory.

This is not an experience reserved for a select few. This is a reality we can all enter into. Consider Enoch. The Scriptures say, "Enoch walked with God; and he was not, for God took him."[1] Enoch was living a supernatural life. He was walking with God in such spectacular victory that he ascended right off the earth. You and I can pursue that same reality in our lives. I'm not saying we're going to be lifted off the earth and taken like Enoch was, but let's not limit God. The same Jesus who walked the earth, healed the sick, raised the dead, and cast out demons is at work in our lives today. We can achieve so much more in our spiritual journey than we understand right now. If we'll put God first, direct our focus—our *kavanah*—toward Him, and obey Him, there is no limit to what we can experience. "With God all things are possible."[2]

It is not a pipe dream to believe that we can walk in supernatural unity with God. Enoch was lifted off the earth supernaturally and taken to be with God because he had reached a place of deep unity with his Creator.

This is our purpose as well—to be one with HaShem just as Yeshua and the Father are one.

In this chapter, I'm going to give you several keys that will help you develop a supernatural walk with your Creator. If you'll apply these truths to your life, you're going to experience a divine reality beyond anything you've known. It will be so apparent your friends and family will notice the difference. And it won't last for a day, a week, a month, or even a year. This reality will be yours until you take your last breath because these keys are not life hacks; they are eternal truths that reveal your very purpose for being here on earth.

Although these keys are powerful, they're simple. The first may seem obvious, but we can't take it for granted if we want to enjoy oneness with God.

ACKNOWLEDGE YOUR CREATOR

Living in supernatural unity with God begins with acknowledging Him. This is not just saying, "I believe in God." It's recognizing that our very lives are a gift from HaShem. Every breath we take is a gift from our Creator, and we must be grateful for this. I have a friend who whenever I ask how he's doing always says, "I'm doing better than I deserve." Friend, every single one of us is doing better than we deserve. We don't even deserve to be here. We didn't do anything that warranted our coming into being. Again, our existence is a gift from our Creator. God gave us the gift of life. He gave of us the gift of being conscious. He gave us the gift of today.

We're only alive because Father God saw fit to make us. God is the Creator, and everything belongs to Him—including our lives. He is the Lord of all, and He reigns over all. So when life is good, we acknowledge God and thank Him. And when we face hardships, we acknowledge God then too.

Job said, "Shall I receive good things from God, but not accept difficulties? Far be it from me."[3] We all need to have that attitude. Life might be hard at times, but that might be exactly what we need. That difficult circumstance may be exactly what is needed to bring spiritual correction in our lives, because the Bible says Father God disciplines every child He receives.[4] So what you're going through right now may be the best thing that could possibly happen to you. It might be painful, but it may be exactly what you need.

Remember the apostle Paul. In 2 Corinthians, he was experiencing a tormenting spirit, a "messenger of Satan,"[5] and he prayed that the Lord would take it away. But God said, "No, Paul, I'm not going to remove it. My grace is sufficient for you, for My power is going to be perfected in your weakness."[6] The hardship was exactly what Paul needed to grow in power and come into spiritual maturity.

You see, Father knew we needed an adversary. He knew we needed a challenge. In the first chapter of Genesis, we read that before God created the world, darkness was moving over the surface of the deep. The darkness was there, but God created man to overcome it. He created us to take dominion over it through the Holy Spirit. This is why Jesus said, "He who overcomes will inherit these things."[7]

We must acknowledge God in everything—the good and the bad—and through faith thank Him for everything that is happening in our lives. That means when we wake up in the morning, before we begin our day, we say, "Father God, thank You that I woke up this morning. Thank You for giving me another day. Father, thank You for using everything that's going to happen today as an opportunity for me to grow in grace and overcome."

If you'll practice recognizing the Lordship of God over the earth and over your life, and if you'll give Father God thanks in all things, believing He is using every struggle to accomplish His will in your life, you'll be well on your way to developing a supernatural platform from which you can ascend into the Spirit of God and walk with your Creator.

RECOGNIZE GOD'S PRESENCE

The second key to walking in unity with God is to discern His presence. Many times as we're moving through life, God is trying to speak to us, but because we're not aware of His presence, we miss the message. We miss His communication. This is why Yeshua said in the Book of Revelation, "He who has an ear, let him hear what the Spirit says."[8] Jesus is speaking to many of His children by His Spirit, but they aren't able to hear His voice.

We need to develop ears to hear and hearts to perceive. In the Old Testament whenever we see Lord rendered in capital letters, it actually represents the original Hebrew letters *yud, hey, vav, hey*—YHWH. Most Semitic scholars believe it is pronounced as a breathy "Yah-weh." This is God's personal, covenant name, and this sacred name is actually written in a verb form that denotes continuous, unfinished action. So within God's name, we see revealed the mystery that Yahweh is always moving.

God is alive. We're not surrounded by empty space. We're surrounded by the Spirit of the Lord, and He is always communicating to us, even when it feels as though He is silent. Remember, Yeshua is called the Word.[9] What does a *word* do? It communicates. If you want to speak to somebody, you use words.

Remember also that in Acts 2, the Ruach HaKodesh, the Spirit of God, fell on those first believers as tongues of fire. God's Spirit could have manifested Himself as a dove as He did at Yeshua's baptism or as a rainbow as He did in the Book of Ezekiel.[10] But He manifested Himself to the first believers as a tongue. Why? It's because a tongue is used to speak, and the Holy Spirit has been given to the church to impart to us the things of God.

Beloved one, the Spirit of God is always speaking to us. He speaks to us through divine intuition. He speaks to us through dreams. He speaks to us in circumstances. He can speak to us through His creation. He can speak

71

to us through other people. But so many times we miss what He's saying because we don't recognize His presence. I want to encourage you. As you're going through your day, be looking for God to speak to you. He's often trying to interrupt us or direct us through our circumstances. Pay attention. Don't be asleep to the working of the Holy Spirit. Be sensitive to His presence.

And don't be stiff-necked; obey Him. If you're feeling a check in your spirit about doing or saying something, don't do it. We all are suffering needlessly to some degree because we don't yield to the Spirit when He is speaking. Although Father God can redeem our mistakes and causes all things to work together for our good, the truth is that many are suffering even now because of unwise financial decisions, marrying the wrong person, or having improper diet habits. These are things that could be avoided if we would listen for the Spirit of God and obey Him when He speaks—even if it is just in a still small voice.

As I shared in my book *Called to Breakthrough*, years ago as I slept one night, I suddenly became intensely aware of the tremendous pain that was in my heart. It wasn't physical, but it hurt. It was a pain that I was not aware was there. It was as if the Lord tore away what normally prevented me from feeling the pain I was carrying and suddenly let me feel it all. In the midst of feeling this very severe pain, I heard an angel say, "You're on the right path."

Then I said to the angel, "If I'm on the right path, why does it hurt so much?"

Then the angel said kindly back to me, "If you would cooperate more, it wouldn't hurt so much."

The reason I tell this story is that it illustrates that we sometimes experience needless pain because we're not following the leading of the Spirit. Beloved one, every day we need to be looking up to God in the Spirit, being sensitive to His voice and asking Him what to do and which way to go.

Whatever you're facing, ask Father, "Are You in this? Is there a lesson I need to learn here? Are You saying something to me in the situation?" As an example, if someone calls you out of the blue, don't just take the call for granted. Ask the Lord, "Are You trying to say something to me through this individual?" Look for His voice in everything.

I also encourage you to pay very close attention to your dreams because Father often speaks to us in our dreams. We read in the Book of Job, "Indeed God speaks once, or twice, yet no one notices it. In a dream, a vision of the night, when sound sleep falls on men, while they slumber in their beds."[11]

As we study Scripture, we see so many times when God gave direction to His loved ones while they were sleeping. Think about Jesus' earthly father, Joseph. How did he know to take Yeshua into Egypt so Herod couldn't kill Him? Father spoke to Joseph in a dream. How did the patriarch Jacob gain the revelation that produced the courage within him to know God was with him? It was revealed to him through a dream.[12]

Pay attention to your dreams. God has saved me

from so many wrong decisions through dreams. And He has directed me and prepared me for so many things through my dreams. But I'm paying attention. I could miss what He wants to tell me if each morning I didn't ask myself, "Did I dream anything last night? Did God say anything to me in my dreams? Did the Spirit give me any messages last night?"

You're not a robot. God is not going to force His Holy Spirit on you. When He speaks, He's not going to put His fist in our faces and say, "You must receive this." No, He's going to reveal Himself to us in love and then give us the choice to listen and respond. Beloved one, we have to listen. We have to be sensitive to God's presence. We must pay attention to the Scriptures and to what we're feeling inside. Oftentimes the Holy Spirit is speaking, but we're not abiding deep enough in the Spirit to hear what He is saying and walk in it. This is why we need to understand God's presence. Until we truly have ears to hear and learn to recognize God's voice, we won't be able to walk in the type of victory Father God has made possible for us.

CLOTHE YOURSELF IN GOD'S NATURE

Third, to walk in supernatural unity with God we must clothe ourselves with His nature. In Galatians 5, Paul reveals the difference between the "clothing" of the Spirit and the clothing of the flesh. He told us to put on the characteristics of the Spirit: "love, joy, peace, patience, kindness, goodness, faithfulness, gentleness, self-control."[13] And he said we are to avoid the traits of the flesh: "immorality, impurity, sensuality, idolatry, sorcery, enmities, strife, jealousy, outbursts of anger, disputes, dissensions, factions, envying, drunkenness, carousing, and things like these."[14] If we're going to walk with God, we need to subdue the nature of the flesh. We need to put it beneath us, refuse to live out of it, and instead put on the garment of the Spirit.

We have a choice in how we respond to the events that happen in our lives. For example, if something frustrates us, we can respond in the flesh with immediate anger, or we can subdue that frustration and respond with kindness, compassion, and love.

The Scriptures say, "For all of you who are being baptized into Christ have clothed yourself with Christ,"[15] and, "Clothe yourselves with compassion, kindness, humility, gentleness and patience."[16] We must make a conscious decision to clothe ourselves with the Lord's nature and not yield to the lust of the flesh or the ambitions of the world. This is not something that automatically happens. We have to intentionally resist the anger, jealousy, frustration, or gossip that might attempt to rise up. We must restrict and subdue the flesh. We have to harness it and instead choose the harder road, which is to take on the nature of Christ.

God's way is always the harder way. To clothe ourselves with Yeshua's nature takes great spiritual strength and discipline because we're swimming upstream. We're swimming against the current. It's a constant battle every minute of every day to not yield to the desires of the flesh and instead choose the straight and narrow way. Yeshua said, "The gate is wide and the way is broad that leads to destruction, and there are many who enter through it. For the gate is small and the way is narrow that leads to life, and there are few who find it."[17] Jesus spoke seven times in Revelation chapters 2 and 3 of the blessings that will come to those who overcome. God made it so we would have to fight. In the natural, resistance helps us build physical strength, and the same is true spiritually. "The testing of your faith [through experience] produces endurance [leading to spiritual maturity, and inner peace]."[18]

Think about this: light is generated through electricity when electrons pass through resistance. The same thing is true in our lives. We have to pass through the resistance of the flesh in order to build the strength to clothe ourselves with the light of God's Spirit. Beloved one, we are called and commissioned to overcome, leading to clothing ourselves with the Spirit of Christ.

There's a spiritual truth I like to call the Law of Similarity and Dissimilarity. The idea behind it is that the more similar we become to something, the more we can know that thing. For example, I can love my dog, but I can't fully know my dog because, for one, I'm not a dog. In a similar way, we can never fully know God until we become like Him. I'm not saying we will become God; I'm saying we're His offspring and are destined to become like Him in our character. The Book of Romans says that "those whom He foreknew, He also predestined to become conformed to the image of His Son."[19]

Father's purpose in our lives is to make us like Yeshua. The more we become like Jesus, the more we take on His nature and experience deep intimacy with Him. To say it a different way, the more we are conformed to His image, the deeper fellowship we will enjoy with Him. As we are transformed into His likeness, we come into unity with God and walk in supernatural victory.

INTERNALIZE GOD'S LOVE

The fourth key is that we need to *internalize Father God's love.* Until you and I become deeply convinced that our Creator, the Master of the universe, really loves us and wants to bless us, we're not going to be able to walk with Him. We may be able to quote Romans 5:8, "But God demonstrates His own love toward us, in that while we were yet sinners, Christ died for us," but do we really have the revelation? Most of us would admit that we haven't fully internalized the reality of the Father's love for us, which led Him to send His Son to die on the cross for our sins.

The truth is that God has been with you in your worst times, and His love for you has never failed. We need to realize God's love for us is unconditional and unchanging. Father wants the best for us. He wants us to be happy. He wants to share Himself with us so we feel what He feels. Until we become convinced that God's favor is toward us and He wants us to experience

His goodness, we won't be able to walk with Him. God is love, and to function in the Spirit, we need to function out of love. That has to begin with understanding how much Father is attached to us.

I've read biographies of great men and women of God who were cutting-edge pioneers of the faith, and yet at the end of their lives they still hadn't internalized the Father's love for them. They had great faith and did great exploits in terms of reaching people with the gospel, but they themselves were never fully convinced Father God loved them. I've been walking with the Lord for forty years, and I still pray daily that Father will help me to understand His love for me. Nothing is more important than this.

Many people study different aspects of God's nature. They have the Scriptures memorized, but deep down inside they don't have an experiential knowledge of how deeply the Father loves and treasures them. And that is such a shame, because to know God's love for us is the most important thing any of us could attain—not just to read about it, have somebody tell us about it, or glibly quote it, but to really internalize the knowledge that we are loved by God. That awareness is absolutely transformative.

We can say, "I believe God loves me." We can quote John 3:16, "God so loved the world, that He gave His only begotten Son, that whoever believes in Him shall not perish, but have eternal life." But some of us have let guilt and shame keep us from internalizing Father's love. We need to understand that Jesus shed His blood to take away our guilt and shame and cleanse our conscience. We are now holy and blameless before Him.[20] Once we repent, we are not to be held hostage by Satan's accusations. We must have confidence that God loves us and nothing will ever separate us from that love.

Why does God love us? To better grasp this mystery, let's go back to the Book of Genesis, which tells us God made man in His own image and likeness. The Creator wanted to form a vessel He could fill with Himself. He created us in His own image so He could give Himself to us. He created you and me so we could receive Him. You see, God is overflowing with goodness, love, kindness, victory, splendor, strength, and power, and He wants to share Himself with us.

We have to become convinced of God's unconditional love for us if we're going to walk with Him. Father God wants us to feel good. He wants us to feel pleasure. He wants us to be happy. Think about your favorite food, how much you enjoy the taste of that dish. Why would HaShem have given us the ability to experience such enjoyment when we eat our favorite foods if He didn't design us to experience pleasure? God wants to make you happy. He wants to lift you up. He wants you to experience His victory. He loves us, and we need to open our heart to internalize our Father's love for us.

El Shaddai, God Almighty, told Abraham, "I am... your exceedingly great reward."[21] Wondrously, God created you and me in His likeness so we could experience His reality. This is what heaven is about: experiencing God's glory. But in order for us to enter into His reality, we have to become truly convinced that He loves us unconditionally, specifically, and personally.

Jesus took the sin out of the way. He took the guilt out of the way. He took the condemnation out of the way. He took the shame out of the way. "There is therefore now no condemnation for those who are in Christ Jesus."[22] There's nothing in the way. We have to open our hearts and realize Father's favor is upon us. He's not angry with us. Our sin is not in the way. God loved you during your worst days, and His love has never failed you. He'll never love you more than He does right now.

Don't Be Afraid to Let Him In

Beloved one, God's love is infinite. The apostle Paul wrote, "For I am convinced that neither death, nor life, nor angels, nor principalities, nor things present, nor things to come, nor powers, nor height, nor depth, nor any other created thing, will be able to separate us from the love of God, which is in Christ Jesus our Lord."[23]

There is nothing that can separate us from this love. In fact, Father designed the whole world for us. And our ultimate purpose and destiny in life is to love Him back.

God is self-existent. He is the beginning, and He is eternal. He has always been. The divine Creator of all does not need anything. But somehow, God has humbled Himself to love and need us. Incredibly, He is drawn to you and me.

If this was not so, would He have sent His Son to experience such agony and even die for us? God's Son was whipped, His beard was pulled out, He had nails put through His hands and feet, and a spear was thrust in His side. He was spat on, mocked, and cursed. If God did not truly love us, would He have put His only begotten Son through such horrendous torment? No. That is how attached to us He is. That is how committed He is to us. Of all of His creation, we are His most precious possession! We are unique. He created us in His likeness so we could receive His love and authentically and truly choose to love Him back. In fact, we are destined to participate in what the Bible calls the marriage supper of the Lamb.[24]

Despite this, we often feel that God is far away. The real issue is not that God is off in the distance and does not see or care. Rather, our real predicament is that we are hesitant to fully open up and completely let Him in.

I remember years ago as a new believer, I had been praying to experience the Lord more deeply. I had already come to faith in Yeshua. I started devotedly reading the Scriptures. I read about the Holy Spirit and had started praying to fully experience Him. One day I was lying on my bed and praying for the Holy Spirit when suddenly I encountered the literal and powerful presence of the Ruach HaKodesh. I felt His person, presence, and manifest power. But do you know what happened next? Even though I was praying for Him to come, something in me pushed Him away when He came. When the Holy Spirit came so near to me, involuntarily, something in me rose up, and I rejected Him. Why? Because He was too close.

You see, we are often afraid to fully let God in to be as close to us as He wants to be because we feel so vulnerable. We are not comfortable with that type of intimacy. We want a relationship with God, but believe it or not, sometimes we prefer Him to be somebody who lives a few doors down. We do not want Him moving into our own bedrooms. We want to partition our lives. We want God to have access to some areas, but then isolate Him so He does not gain full possession of us. We do not want Him having free access into our whole lives and be so close and personal. We say we want Him, but the truth is, we do not want Him to be as imminent as He wants to be. It makes us feel too exposed, and the familiarity can frightens us.

Furthermore, we are reluctant to fully open up and let God in to have absolute control. We are hesitant to be that accountable. We want our own freedom. And to let Him into the very center of our being would mean that we would have to fully surrender control of our lives to Him. Some of us are not fully ready to do so. There is something in our fleshly nature that resists it.

Beloved one, we have to recognize and surrender to the reality of how close God is. We need to remove any barriers that we have established that hinder His love and involvement in our lives. Yeshua said, "Behold, I stand at the door and knock; if anyone hears My voice and opens the door, I will come in to him and will dine with him, and he with Me."[25]

Let's pray together to invite Father God to come in and make Himself at home in our lives.

Father, right now, in Yeshua's name, I pray that You would soften and open our hearts so that we would create a place of intimacy for You within us that is deeper than we have ever experienced. Father, I pray that You would expand our hearts. Help us to embrace that You are not somewhere else; You are right here with us. Father, I ask You to open every heart now that wants You in a deeper way. We ask You for the grace to not be afraid of You and to trust You enough to give You control. Unlock the door of our hearts to not fear intimacy, to not push You back. Help us receive You into the depths of our souls so You can fully make Your home within us (John 14:23). In Yeshua's name.

If we're truly going to ascend upward and walk in victory with Yeshua, we have to understand that no matter where we live in the world or what our occupation is, our purpose is the same: to be transformed into Yeshua's likeness and come into unity with Him. We may be different ages and in different seasons of life, but we all have the same destination: to come into unity with Father God through the love that is in His Son, Messiah Jesus. This is the reason we're here on planet Earth.

Please don't take these truths lightly:

- Acknowledge your Creator.

- Recognize God's presence.

- Clothe yourself in God's nature.

- Internalize God's love.

- Don't be afraid to let Him in.

These insights may be simple, but the simplest truths are oftentimes the weightiest and most profound. Commit to reviewing these principles until practicing them becomes second nature. If you do, I am confident you will be blessed and God's abiding presence and joy will, more and more, become your portion.

Chapter 7

LIVE FOR ETERNITY

ABOUT FORTY YEARS ago, just a few years after I accepted Yeshua, I had an extremely powerful and life-changing encounter with the Lord in my sleep. In this vision of the night,[1] I was standing in the attic of a home. It was a very simple room, rectangular in shape, and it appeared to be about thirty feet long and twelve feet wide. There was a window on both sides, and it was dark. There were other people in the attic with me, and we were standing against the back wall.

Suddenly, from one of the two windows came an incredibly beautiful stream of light that contained all the colors of the rainbow. It was flowing like a river through the window and was unlike anything I'd ever seen. The best way I can describe it is to say it loosely resembled living, multidimensional crepe paper that looked to be about a foot and a half high. Again, it was a beautiful spirit of flowing life containing all the colors of the rainbow.

I stepped away from the back wall and moved toward the window where the rainbow light was flowing in from. When I reached the window, I stuck my head outside, and everywhere I looked there was vibrant color. It was an eternity of color. In the vision/dream, I opened my arms and said, "Come and live inside me!" And then I immediately heard the audible voice of God deep down in what felt like the center of my belly, and He said one word: *eternity.*

Beloved one, we are called to live for eternity.

Oftentimes, when people think of eternity, they define it as a length of time that goes on forever. But that is not a full understanding. Eternity isn't just a measure of time; it's a quality of life. Jesus said, "This is eternal life, that they may know You, the only true God, and Jesus Christ whom You have sent."[2] So Yeshua defined eternity as a state in which we are in union with God.

Our Father is eternal, and to know Him is to experience eternal life. Eternity exists outside time, space, and the material world that surrounds us. But too many of us are not living with an eternal perspective. We're only living for the here and now. Our eyes are set on the things of the world, and we're pursuing the things of the world.

The Scriptures say, "Our citizenship is in heaven, from which also we eagerly wait for a Savior, the Lord Jesus Christ."[3] If we're going to live as citizens of heaven, who are *in this world but not of it*, we need to understand reality not just from the perspective of the here and the now but from the eternal. And to get an eternal perspective, our minds need to be completely rewired.

What we see happening around us is transitory. This world is passing away. As the Scriptures say, "The grass withers, the flower fades, but the word of our God stands forever."[4] When our minds are renewed through the written Word of God and communion with the Spirit, we're brought into a new dimension of light and we can exclaim with the psalmist, "In Your light we see light."[5] We can see that what we experience on a daily basis due to our circumstances is temporal and we no longer have to respond as if it's the only thing that matters. We are not overwhelmed by the "now" because we have an eternal perspective.

Consider with me the different experiences of two people observing a parade in their city. One person is standing on the sidewalk as the marching bands, drumlines, and vintage cars go by. He waves as the floats carrying the mayor and other politicians pass by. He scurries for the candy being tossed by business leaders riding in the beds of pickup trucks decorated with balloons. As this individual on the sidewalk is watching the parade, he is taking in only one scene at a time. When the marching band is in front of him, he sees only the marching band until it passes. He doesn't see the balloons or the local businessmen tossing candy until they are immediately before him.

But let's now think about an individual viewing the same parade from a hot air balloon three thousand feet above the ground. As the person in the hot air balloon looks down on the parade, she does not take it in one scene at a time. She sees the entire parade all at once from beginning to end. She sees the whole picture and has a totally different perspective from the person watching from the ground, who is only experiencing one small thing at a time.

So it should be with us. Our perception of life must be based on more than what is happening in this current season of our lives, as if the present moment is all there is. We need to have an eternal vantage point.

MOMENTARY, LIGHT AFFLICTIONS

The apostle Paul even understood that through his trials, God was imparting in him something of eternal significance. In fact, he said: "For momentary, light affliction is producing for us an eternal weight of glory far beyond all comparison, while we look not at the things which are seen, but at the things which are not seen; for the things which are seen are temporal, but the things which are not seen are eternal."[6]

Paul had been imprisoned, beaten, shamed, persecuted, rejected, shipwrecked, and whipped. If he didn't know the Lord and have an eternal perspective, he would have seen himself as a victim. But he said, "These are momentary, light afflictions; they're passing away; and my identity isn't defined by these trials because I have citizenship in heaven. And these momentary, light afflictions are actually producing in me the weight of eternity."

Paul saw the imprisonment, the beatings, the torture, the shame, the rejection, and the suffering as temporary winds that would soon pass him by. And he knew that by going through the challenges, glory from another realm was being wrought within him.

Paul had an eternal perspective, and that is what we're also being called to. We can't interpret our lives just by what is going on in this instant. We must keep our eyes on eternity and realize that any temporary suffering we endure is imparting something to us that is far greater.

When athletes have the goal of becoming Olympic

gold medalists, they will go through an excruciating training schedule. Some of them wake up at four o'clock in the morning and train nine hours a day. They put their bodies through tremendous strain, but they endure it because they know the temporary pain of training is not worthy to be compared with the feeling of winning a gold medal in the Olympic Games.

Paul lived his life looking toward the eternal reward he would receive. You and I need to likewise be living with a view toward eternity. This world is not our home. "For all that is in the world, the lust of the flesh and the lust of the eyes and the boastful pride of life, is not from the Father, but is from the world."[7] We are strangers and aliens on the earth.[8] Our citizenship is in heaven. We're in the world but not of it.

Paul didn't get his perception of reality from the visible world because he knew what he could see in the world around him was temporal. In fact, the Scriptures say that everything we see right now in the visible world is going to be burned up in fire.[9] It's all going to be done away with, and God is going to bring forth something brand new, where the first will be last and the last will be first.[10] So we need to start asking ourselves, "What is God wanting from me during my time on this earth? How can I have an attitude like Moses had, who lived in this world as one who knew he was not of it?"

Moses had everything the world could offer yet was looking for the eternal inheritance that came from his Creator, an inheritance that was not of this realm. The Book of Hebrews records that "Moses, when he had grown up, refused to be called the son of Pharaoh's daughter, choosing rather to endure ill-treatment with the people of God than to enjoy the passing pleasures of sin, considering the reproach of Christ greater riches than the treasures of Egypt; for he was looking to the reward."[11]

A Radical Rewiring

Perhaps as you're reading this, you agree intellectually with what I'm saying. But it's not enough to intellectually agree with these truths. We must let them change the way we live. We can't spend our lives just pursuing pleasure. We can't keep God in a little compartmentalized box. That is not living for eternity.

Living for eternity calls for a radical rewiring of our minds that causes us to consciously live every day with the awareness that we belong to HaShem and our life purpose is bound up in Him alone. Every day is a day to be overcoming—to war against the powers of darkness so we are victorious over our old nature and, more and more, are transformed by the renewing of our minds. This is why Yeshua continually calls His chosen ones to overcome: "To him who overcomes, I will grant to eat of the tree of life which is in the Paradise of God."[12]

We're in the world to bring forth the light of Yeshua. But how can we share the reality of eternity with others if we're not captured by it ourselves? If we haven't brought eternity into our own lives, how are we going to impact those around us with the reality that Jesus is coming again soon?

Beloved one, it's time to take an inventory of our lives. What are our priorities? Are the words that we are speaking pleasing to God? How are we using money? How are we employing our talents? How much time are we devoting to the Lord through His Word, prayer, and worship as compared to how much time we are spending watching secular YouTube, television, or streaming services? How are we actually living out our lives?

Along this same line, if we're truly following Yeshua, we should be getting some blowback from the world because the Word says, "All who desire to live godly in Christ Jesus will be persecuted."[13] Why? Because those who are living by the power of eternity are on a radically different trajectory than those who are living by the power of this present age.

We need to be totally rewired so it becomes evident to God and everyone around us that we are citizens of the kingdom of heaven. We are living by the powers of the *age to come* as we wait for the glory of Yeshua to be revealed.

But let's be honest with ourselves. Many of us who call ourselves believers are much worldlier than we allow ourselves to think we are. Most in the Western world are outward-focused, trying to fulfill themselves with the world. Several years ago, I had a prophetic dream that really drove this point home.

In the dream, I was ministering at a congregation I once pastored, and while I was preaching, everyone suddenly stood up and started reciting the Pledge of Allegiance. It was so loud it drowned out my message. Humiliated, I left the pulpit and hid in the restroom.

I said, "Lord, I feel so embarrassed. What should I do?" The Lord answered, "Go back in there and finish." I really did not want to go back in, but I obeyed. As I walked behind the pulpit, somebody yelled out, "They don't want to listen to you anymore!" I finished the message, and the dream ended.

Shaken by this dream, I asked the Lord the next morning, "What did I do wrong to bring this about? Where have I been weak as a leader that such a thing could happen? Where did I fail?" Several days later as I was praying about this dream, still disturbed by it, the Holy Spirit suddenly spoke to me: "It was not about you being a weak leader. I was not showing you this to point out something you are doing wrong. I was showing you that My people's allegiance is not really to Me; their allegiance is to the American dream."

Here were all these people gathered in a congregation thinking they were "true" followers of Yeshua, and yet they were totally deceived. Deep down inside, their allegiance was not to the Lord. They weren't motivated enough to fully live for Him or submit to His authority upon their lives. They didn't want to surrender everything to Him or suffer for the sake of the kingdom. Instead, they were trying to hang on to this life. They used God and included Him in their lives when it was convenient, but they did not belong to Jesus. Their life's focus was to pursue the American dream and all they thought it offered.

Paul, on the other hand, was abandoned to God. In fact, he said he had suffered the loss of all things in order to gain Christ: "But whatever things were gain to me, those things I have counted as loss for the sake of Christ. More than that, I count all things to be loss in view of the surpassing value of knowing Christ Jesus my Lord, for whom I have suffered the loss of all things, and count them but rubbish so that I may gain Christ."[14]

Hearing Yeshua's words in Matthew 7:22–23 puts the fear of God in me: "Many will say to Me on that day, 'Lord, Lord, did we not prophesy in Your name, and in Your name cast out demons, and in Your name perform many miracles?' And then I will declare to them, 'I never knew you; depart from Me.'"[15] In other words, upon Jesus' return, there will be many people who thought they belonged to Him, and Yeshua is going to say, "I never knew you." Why? They thought they were Christians, but they had never been transformed. They were living for the present age and not for the kingdom of God and the age to come.

I'm living for Yeshua. That's what my whole life is about. And baruch HaShem (bless the Lord), if I die, that's even better, because I'll be in heaven with Him. "To live is Christ and to die is gain."[16] I'm not living for this world. I'm not putting my family first. I'm not even putting my children first. I'm not putting my occupation first. I'm not putting success first. I'm not putting my possessions first. Anything I lose in this life is not worthy to be compared with knowing Yeshua and the power of His resurrection and the fellowship of His suffering. If I lost everything, I would still be OK because I would still have Him! Like the apostle Paul, I say, "To live is Christ and to die is gain."

In the last chapter of God's Word, Jesus said, "Behold, I am coming quickly, and My reward is with Me, to render to every man according to what he has done."[17] Beloved one, we must live not expecting to be fully rewarded in this life. The fullness of our reward will be realized in the age to come. Jesus said, "When you give to the poor, do not sound a trumpet before you, as the hypocrites do in the synagogues and in the streets, so that they may be honored by men. Truly I say to you, they have their reward in full. But when you give to the poor, do not let your left hand know what your right hand is doing, so that your giving will be in secret; and your Father who sees what is done in secret will reward you."[18] Even a cup of cold water given in Yeshua's name is going to be rewarded when He comes again and we're revealed in glory with Him.[19]

Jesus is coming soon. Let's not live for the here and now; let's live for eternity.

In Jewish culture, we pray what is cxalled the Shema, the ancient prayer found in Deuteronomy 6 that has become the central declaration of the Jewish faith. It begins, "Sh'ma Yisra'el! Adonai Eloheinu, Adonai echad,"[20] which translated means, "Hear, O Israel: The Lord is our God. The Lord is one!"[21] The word *sh'ma* doesn't simply mean to hear with our ears; it means to hear and obey.

Beloved one, Father God isn't calling us simply to hear His truth; He's calling us to hear and obey—to put it into practice. That is why in the pages that follow I have included one hundred devotional meditations that will help us continue our quest to enter God's presence by communing with Him daily through His Word.

The Spirit and the Word are one. The Word gives us the foundation upon which our faith is built, and the Spirit illuminates the mysteries of God, giving us fresh revelation of His truth.[22]

So let us now turn our attention to connecting with the Lord by affirming the truth in His Word.

It is the Spirit who gives life; the flesh profits nothing; the words that I have spoken to you are spirit and are life.[23]

BE CONFIDENT IN GOD'S LOVE

But God demonstrates His own love toward us, in
that while we were yet sinners, Christ died for us.
—ROMANS 5:8

PAUL'S WORDS REMIND us of a fundamental truth: God loves us so much that while we were still sinners, He sent Jesus to die for us. Think about this for a minute. When we were in a totally degenerate state, not looking for God or even thinking about Him, Father God sent His Son to redeem and save us. When we had nothing to our credit, God loved us, and He loves us with this same love every second of every day.

This is so important to remember because sometimes, somehow along the way we can start to think God's love for us depends on our works. Subtly we begin to believe God loves us if we are obedient enough. But the reality is that even while we were still dead in our transgressions and sins, God sent His Son to die in our place simply because He loves us.

And today's good news is that His love for us will never change. He'll never love you any more or less than He does right now. If God loved you even when you were estranged from Him, you can be confident that He loves you right now and He'll love you for the rest of eternity.

Beloved one, let's open our hearts and, though the enemy does not want us to, receive God's unconditional grace and love into our lives. This involves making a conscious decision to believe.

Day 2

HE WILL SET YOU FREE

The Spirit of the Lord God is upon me, because the Lord
has anointed me to bring good news to the afflicted;
He has sent me to bind up the brokenhearted, to pro-
claim liberty to captives and freedom to prisoners.
—Isaiah 61:1

GOD IS THE most tender, loving person in the universe.

Father God sent Yeshua into the world because of His compassion for us. He yearns to touch us, heal us, repair us, and love us—individually, personally, and directly. Thus, Isaiah prophesied that the Messiah would bind up the brokenhearted and proclaim liberty to captives. In Luke 4, Jesus began His ministry by reading from Isaiah 61 and, attributing this prophecy to Himself, said, "Today this Scripture has been fulfilled in your hearing."[1]

Beloved one, Yeshua is the same yesterday, today, and forever. He is currently delivering the oppressed and proclaiming liberty to those who are bound. Whatever in your heart has been broken, let Yeshua heal you. He is alive and with you now. Open your heart completely to Him, and He will set you free.

One of my favorite portions of Scripture is where Yeshua says, "And you will know the truth, and the truth will make you free....So if the Son makes you free, you will be free indeed."[2] We have been called to glory. Our destiny is to feel and experience God's bliss. As the ancient Westminster Catechism states, "Man's chief end is to glorify God, and to enjoy him for ever."[3]

MAKE TIME FOR HIM

She had a sister called Mary, who was seated at the Lord's feet, listening to His word. But Martha was distracted with all her preparations; and she came up to Him and said, "Lord, do You not care that my sister has left me to do all the serving alone? Then tell her to help me." But the Lord answered and said to her, "Martha, Martha, you are worried and bothered about so many things; but only one thing is necessary, for Mary has chosen the good part, which shall not be taken away from her."
—LUKE 10:39–42

IT IS ESSENTIAL that we spend time alone with God. Often we do not know what is going on in our soul because we are so busy and distracted. Whether it is work, relationships, or social media, we are so connected to the outside world that we are not always in touch with what is happening inside our hearts. But when we spend time alone with God, allowing Him access, we are forced to face what is going on inside.

Sometimes this can be painful, but we need to allow ourselves to feel our exhaustion, fear, and hopelessness, and then share it with the Father. He will come in and fill those places, and we will begin to rise up and be made whole.

Beloved one, let us give ourselves completely to the things that will bring us into a deeper relationship with Yeshua and avoid the things that will draw us away from Him.

THE GOD OF ALL COMFORT

*Blessed be the God and Father of our Lord Jesus
Christ, the Father of mercies and God of all comfort, who comforts us in all our affliction.*
—2 CORINTHIANS 1:3–4

HAVE YOU EVER noticed that sometimes when
you're going through the hardest circumstances—
for example, when you've suffered a great loss or when
something happens that upends your life—the peace of
God is more profound?

I remember years ago being thrown out of my parents' house. My decision to follow Jesus caused a lot
of division and chaos in my family. As you may know,
it's anathema in the Jewish community for a Jew to
believe in Jesus. You would think it was devastating to
be kicked out of my parents' house, but the next day
when I looked around, I felt like the entire world was
bathed in a blanket of peace. I hardly have the words to
describe it. Somehow God imparted His presence to me
in such a way that it rewired my psyche so that the next
day, everything I looked at was cover by an amazing,
supernatural blanket of God's love and peace.

Beloved one, we don't know what we're going to face
in the future. We don't know what difficulties may
come our way, but I want to tell you this: God is going
to be there. He will always be faithful to you, and He
will always be with you to comfort you. You will overcome the world.[1]

DON'T BE RULED BY
YOUR EMOTIONS

Then Jesus was led up by the Spirit into the wilderness to be tempted by the devil.
—MATTHEW 4:1

HOW WE FEEL is kind of like the weather—we can't control it. To be strong in the Lord, we have to learn to operate in the Spirit, in the Word, and in faith, regardless of how we're feeling.

Until we learn to operate by our will rather than being controlled by our emotions and circumstances, we'll never become mature sons and daughters of God. In fact, the Lord will bring us into challenging circumstances that force us to rise above our emotions just to train us.

After Yeshua was baptized in the Jordan River, the Spirit of God immediately led Him into the wilderness, where He was assaulted by the devil for forty days. Jesus felt tired, hungry, and weak. *But He rose above how He felt* and resisted every temptation. As a result of this, He came out of the wilderness in the power the Ruach HaKodesh.

I want to encourage you today to be strong. Rise up and be a warrior. Practice exercising your will and trusting God and His Word, even when you're facing challenging circumstances and difficult emotions. Let's practice His presence at all times. When we do this during times of testing, we'll be made strong. Like Yeshua, we must resist the forces of darkness in order to be fortified. And when you and I get strong, beloved one, we'll be happy.

THE SOURCE OF GREATNESS

*Your right hand upholds me; and Your gen-
tleness makes me great.*
—PSALM 18:35

DAVID IS ONE of the most beloved personalities in
Scripture. One reason many people are drawn to
him is that David is so relatable. This legendary king of
Israel had strengths and weaknesses, just as we do. As
most of us know, David committed adultery with Bathsheba, even putting her husband on the front line to be
killed in battle so he could take his wife. David's choices
reveal some real flaws that indicate he was an imperfect
human being.

David fell at times in his walk with the Lord, just as
we sometimes do. Yet he knew it was God who held
him up. He realized his greatness came from the Lord's
gentleness toward him. I love the imagery of John 13:23,
when John was leaning on Jesus' bosom. I think of how
safe and secure John must have felt in Yeshua's gentle
love. Even when David fell, Father never forsook him.
David was disciplined and suffered for his sin, but God's
lovingkindness toward him was constant.

It was Father God's gentleness and faithfulness toward
David that made him so special, not David's own goodness or ingenuity, and the same is true of us. When we
fall, we "will not be hurled headlong, because the Lord
is the One who holds [our] hand."[1] Beloved one, God
loves us despite our faults and failings, and when we
repent, He will restore us. His gentleness makes us great.

HE IS ALREADY IN YOU!

For indeed, the kingdom of God is within you.
—Luke 17: 21

MANY YEARS AGO, I was intently seeking the Lord to experience more of Him. I tried everything I knew to do, but nothing seemed to work. Finally, one day the Holy Spirit spoke to me and said, "You're not finding Me because you are searching for Me on the outside, as if what you are doing will make you experience Me. I want you to stop focusing on things that are on the outside and instead ask Me to give you revelation of the fact that *I am already in you*." From the moment I received that revelation, a fresh power came into my life, and I have never been the same.

So many of us aren't experiencing God's power and presence because we are only looking for Him in the world outside us. Father God does speak to us through supernatural signs in the material world, just as He spoke to Moses in a burning bush.[1] But that's not primarily where we will experience Him. He foundationally speaks to us from within.

Beloved one, if we are primarily relying on circumstances and signs in the outer world to guide us, we will be deceived. The enemy can manipulate the natural world too.[2] To experience the unfathomable depths of God, we must focus on being led by the inner witness of the Holy Spirit and embrace the truth that *Jesus is already inside us*!

Day 8

A REASON TO REJOICE

I pray that the eyes of your heart may be enlightened, so that you will know what is the hope of His calling, what are the riches of the glory *of His inheritance in the saints.*
—EPHESIANS 1:18, EMPHASIS ADDED

GOD'S CALL ON our lives is so glorious, Paul's prayer here is asking Father to open the eyes of our hearts so you and I can comprehend this. The hope of our calling is to be glorified with Jesus, be conformed to His image, and live forever in heaven. This eternal plan of God for you and me is so incredible that if we fully grasped it, we would be smiling from ear to ear every single day.

I know life can be hard. Pain and oppression are all around us, but we must remember this world is not our home. We are so valuable to God that He sent His Son into the world to be nailed to the cross in order to purchase us for Himself. Yeshua is coming back, and "eye has not seen, nor ear heard, nor have entered into the heart of man the things which God has prepared for those who love Him."[1]

Beloved one, you and I have a reason to rejoice. We're going home! We're going to a place that's better than anything we could ever dream. Let's not lose sight of this eternal reality. Let's look up and be glad. Our redemption draws nigh.

ROOT YOURSELF IN HIM

He shall be like a tree planted by the rivers of water,
that brings forth its fruit in its season, whose leaf also
shall not wither; and whatever he does shall prosper.
—PSALM 1:3

WHEN GOD IS our source, no matter what's happening around us, we're going to be fruitful because Yeshua said, "He who abides in Me and I in him, he bears much fruit."[1] This is why we must aim to root ourselves in God, because when we do, we can go deep into the waters of eternal life.

You see, God's Spirit dwells beneath the surface. The atmosphere of the Spirit is complete peace, just as in the natural the environment at the floor of the ocean is calm. Even if there's a huge storm on the surface of the ocean, everything is still at the bottom. The same is true of the deep places in God's Spirit. As we choose to draw near to Him daily, the roots of our faith go deeper and deeper until we tap into a continual river of His living water and shalom. When we draw from this well, God's peace and goodness can flow out of us regardless of what's happening on the surface of our lives.

Beloved one, if we put Jesus first, we can be fruitful in HaShem no matter what we face. "The God of peace will soon crush Satan under your feet."[2] So let's put aside the distractions and truly make Yeshua Lord.

Day 10

KEEP YOUR HEART FIXED ON YESHUA

This is the confidence which we have before Him, that, if we ask anything according to His will, He hears us. And if we know that He hears us in whatever we ask, we know that we have the requests which we have asked from Him.
—1 JOHN 5:14–15

SOMETIMES PEOPLE THINK if they believe, they can have anything they want—the fancy car, the big house, the grand trips and nice clothes. Even if they don't intend to, they see Jesus as a magic genie and view their relationship with Him as a means to achieve the American dream.

But the Bible says God grants us everything we ask for *that's according to His will.* Yes, He wants us to be happy, but He wants us to be happy from being made whole in Yeshua. When Messiah walked the earth, He had inner contentment and was completely at peace. It wasn't because He had the biggest house, ate the finest food, or rode the best donkey. This wholeness was something that He possessed inside Himself because the kingdom of God is within.

Beloved one, I want to encourage you to ask Father God to draw you into a relationship with Him that will bring you into contentment, peace, and wholeness. Ask Father to help you keep your heart fixed on Yeshua. You don't have to scream for it. If you just pray with simple, childlike faith, seeking the giver and not the gift, you can have confidence He will answer that prayer.

COUNT IT ALL JOY

My brethren, count it all joy when you fall into various trials, knowing that the testing of your faith produces patience. But let patience have its perfect work, that you may be perfect and complete, lacking nothing.
—JAMES 1:2–4, NKJV

THINK ABOUT A child in his mother's womb, totally encased in loving-kindness. The mother is carrying her baby in a secret place, where the child is protected from the outer world.

Beloved one, that is how God loves you and me. I know it doesn't always feel that way. Life can be difficult, even painful. When we face hardships and heartaches, the question becomes, If God cares so much, why does He not do something to take away these challenges?

Father allows His children to face difficulty because He uses the obstacles and hardships to bring us into maturity. When the Lord sent some type of satanic resistance in Paul's pathway, he prayed, "Lord, remove this difficulty." What was the Lord's reply? "My grace is sufficient for you."[1]

In order to mature as sons and daughters of God, we must go through adversity. God doesn't want us to stay infants. A baby's love is based on an attachment because of receiving. But a mature person chooses to love not just for what they can get but for what they can give. Together, may we grow up in the Lord and fulfill His plans for our lives!

Day 12

ANOINTED TO SERVE

*And He opened the book and found the place where
it was written, "The Spirit of the Lord is upon
Me, because He anointed Me to preach the gospel
to the poor...to set free those who are oppressed, to
proclaim the favorable year of the Lord."*
—LUKE 4:17–19, EMPHASIS ADDED

IN TODAY'S VERSE, Yeshua said the Spirit of the Lord
had anointed Him *to*... Anointings come to equip us
to fulfill a purpose. Jesus was anointed to preach, set
free, and reveal God's favor. So I want to ask you today,
What are you anointed for?

The Bible says the Spirit has given each of us some
type of spiritual gift we can use to serve others.[1] If you
don't know how you are anointed to serve, ask Father
God to show you. Ask Him what specific gifts, talents,
or strengths He has imparted to you. When Father God
shows you how He has anointed you, ask yourself, "How
can I use this anointing to serve the Lord by serving the
body of Jesus? What is my assignment?"

All of us are called to serve. Many people are only
receiving, but following Yeshua is about more than
being filled up with more of Him. It's also about letting
Him pour Himself out to others through us. Jesus said
the one who serves is greater than the one who is served.
So, beloved one, let's identify our anointing, and then
let's step out and serve people.

ONLY ONE WAY

*I am the way, and the truth, and the life; no
one comes to the Father but through Me.*
—JOHN 14:6

TODAY MORE THAN ever before, people are refusing to accept that Jesus is the only way to eternal life. The antichrist spirit is the instigator of this deception that is causing more and more people to believe it is unreasonable and ignorant to believe Jesus is the only way to heaven. They say, "People can go to God any way they choose; there are many paths. Who are you to say your way is the only one?"

The Scriptures are clear: "he who believes in the Son has eternal life; but he who does not obey the Son will not see life, but the wrath of God abides on him."[1] Those who hold to the Bible's teaching on this point find themselves outside the mainstream. And due to demonic and cultural pressure, many followers of Yeshua are shrinking back in fear from taking a stand.

Yeshua declared, "Enter through the narrow gate; for the gate is wide and the way is broad that leads to destruction, and there are many who enter through it."[2] Beloved one, narrow is the path for those of us who maintain the conviction that there is no other way to be saved from our sins and go to heaven except through Messiah Jesus. Today more than ever before, we must draw a line in the sand and resolve to stand and be His witnesses.

GOD WANTS TO BE CLOSE TO YOU

If anyone loves Me, he will keep My word; and
My Father will love him, and We will come
to him and make Our abode with him.
—JOHN 14:23

DESPITE LONGING TO be close to Father God, we often feel that He is far away. But the real issue is not that God is far off and doesn't care about us. Our real predicament is that we are hesitant to open up and completely let Him in.

Years ago, as a new believer, I was praying to experience the Lord more deeply. One day, in my bedroom, suddenly I encountered the powerful presence of the Ruach HaKodesh. But you know what happened next? Something in me pushed Him away. When the Holy Spirit came so close and near to me, involuntarily something in me rose up, and I rejected Him. Why? Because He was too close.

You see, we are often afraid to fully let God in because we feel vulnerable. We are not comfortable with that type of intimacy. We want a relationship with God, but sometimes we prefer Him to be somebody who lives a few doors down. We don't want Him moving into our own bedrooms.

Beloved one, we need to recognize and surrender to the reality of how close God is. We need to remove any barriers we have established that hinder His love and involvement in our lives. Let's ask Father to expand our hearts so He can fully make His home within us.

Day 15

CELEBRATE AND REJOICE!

Rejoice in the Lord always; again I will say, rejoice!
—PHILIPPIANS 4:4

YESHUA'S FIRST MIRACLE in the Gospel of John was turning water into wine at a wedding celebration. What does this teach us? For one, this reveals to us that our God is happy and joyful. I believe Jesus performed His first miracle in an atmosphere of celebration as a way of calling us to walk in an attitude of happiness and victory by practicing rejoicing.

The challenges we face here on earth make it easy for us to become negative, but God is calling us to swim upstream. Instead of letting the trials of life get us down, He wants us to practice rejoicing because the joy of the Lord is our strength.[1]

Not many years ago, the Lord spoke audibly to my spirit, and I clearly heard Him say: "Rejoice continually, and you'll overcome every obstacle." One of the ways we rejoice continually is by knowing that our difficulties are going to pass and we will overcome. The Lord wants us to rejoice in the midst of whatever we're facing, knowing that we're going to come out of it shining even more brightly because "God causes all things to work together for good to those who love God, to those who are called according to His purpose."[2]

So, beloved one, break off everything that would cause you to be discouraged and sad. Rejoice continually, and you'll overcome every obstacle. Our God is happy, and He's calling us to a joyful, celebratory life in Him.

Day 16

SPIRITUAL BREAKTHROUGH

...Christ in you, the hope of glory.
—Colossians 1:27

BREAKTHROUGH COMES IN two primary forms: circumstantial and spiritual. Breakthrough in our circumstances is important, but it can only bring temporary contentment.

Years ago I was going through a very difficult time. I had wrestled all through high school and built my whole identity around it. But when I graduated and walked off the wrestling mat for the last time, I suddenly felt lost.

As I sat in our family room one day, I looked out the window and felt a deep sense of emptiness inside. My circumstances had changed, and who I was seemed to have disappeared with them. I looked outside at the lovely nature. But you know what? It couldn't do anything for me. Because my soul was lost and confused, nothing on the outside made a difference.

Our circumstances are like the scenery outside a window. There are some circumstances that we enjoy, but at the deepest level they really can't do anything for us. They are part of the material world, and our deepest needs can only be met by God, who is Spirit.[1] If we are only looking for breakthrough in our circumstances, we will come up empty. Thus, the real key to abundant life is getting breakthrough in the spirit! How do we get this breakthrough? By drawing ourselves out of that which exists in the material world and pressing into the reality of *Christ in us, the hope of glory.*

EVIDENCE OF FAITH

You have faith and I have works; show me your faith without the works, and I will show you my faith by my works.
—JAMES 2:18

IT IS TRUE that we are saved by grace and not works.[1] But if we have the Spirit of God living inside us, there will be Holy Spirit-inspired actions. True, biblical faith will produce fruit—it is the natural consequence of being alive in Christ.

This is why the Bible says we should examine ourselves and see if we're in the faith.[2] We should always be taking inventory to see if our lifestyle reflects our faith. If we say we believe one thing, but our actions are contradictory, what we say is discredited, and the gospel gets a black eye. So we must ask ourselves, "Do I treat people with love and respect? Do I reach out to help others? Am I using my talents to build the kingdom? Am I feeding on the Word?" These are all works that demonstrate our faith is alive in Yeshua.

Beloved one, our challenge is to make our lifestyle congruent with what we say we believe. If it is, then we should be encouraged that our faith is growing. But if it's not, we need to repent and make some soul corrections so our words, thoughts, actions—every part of our lives—come into alignment with biblical faith, which involves not just what we believe but also who we are and what we do.

Day 18

HE IS WITH YOU

*No temptation has overtaken you but such as is
common to man; and God is faithful, who will
not allow you to be tempted beyond what you are
able, but with the temptation will provide the way of
escape also, so that you will be able to endure it.*
—1 CORINTHIANS 10:13

WHEN WE'RE IN the midst of being tempted, God is with us. When you're in the middle of losing your temper, having a bad attitude, fighting lust—whatever it is—God is right with you. His love for you does not change, and He is going to give you a way of escape as you keep clinging to Him in the midst of the temptation.

You may feel like you're failing. You might be thinking, "Yes, I'm clinging to God, but I'm still sinning. My attitude is still bad. My words are still not fully in alignment with God's love." But if you'll keep hanging on to God, if you'll keep praying in the middle of the situation, God is going to strengthen you through the process, and you are going to overcome.

God is perfecting us, and He is going to complete the work He started in us. Whatever temptation or challenge we're dealing with, we will overcome it. God will make a way out. It may not happen in a moment. There may be a process involved, but we will overcome because we are born of His Spirit and victors in Yeshua.

Day 19

AN ABUNDANCE OF COMFORT

For just as the sufferings of Christ are ours in abun-
dance, so also our comfort is abundant through Christ.
—2 CORINTHIANS 1:5

THERE'S NO WAY around it: being a disciple of Jesus involves suffering. "Indeed," Paul wrote, "all who desire to live godly in Christ Jesus will be persecuted."[1] We will face hardship, heartache, and hurt because of our faith in Yeshua. So we need to put on the armor of a soldier and set our faith and teeth toward the wind, recognizing that we're going to take a few hits. This is part of what it means to follow Jesus.

Notice, however, that today's verse goes on to say that our comfort also is abundant through Christ Jesus. In other words, when we're following Messiah Jesus, we're going to face situations that cause us tremendous grief. But in the midst of the pain, God is going to bless us, and we will receive a supernatural impartation of comfort through the ministry of the Ruach HaKodesh.

Beloved one, be confident that whatever trial, persecution, or difficulty you might encounter from now until the end of your life on earth, you're never alone. God loves you and me with an eternal love, and He's always watching over us. Night and day, He's continuously shepherding our souls.

As you follow Him, Father God will make Himself known to you, and you will experience His comfort even through the hardships you will walk through in life.

LOVE BIG

He who sows sparingly will also reap sparingly, and
he who sows bountifully will also reap bountifully.
—2 CORINTHIANS 9:6

HAVE YOU EVER heard heavenly music in your sleep? That has happened to me maybe five times in my life where in my sleep I heard music too wonderful to describe. It was music unlike anything I've ever heard in this world. I love music in this world, but the music I've heard a few times in my sleep is indescribable.

One time when this happened I was in Zambia, and that particular time I heard these words in the music: "Love big and take out the decimal point." I felt like the Lord was telling me to love big, give big, and live big. In 2 Corinthians 9:6, Paul says, "He who sows sparingly will also reap sparingly, and he who sows bountifully will also reap bountifully."

So I want to encourage you today, beloved one, to trust God—live big, love big, give big, and expect big things from God. You're more than you think you are. And God wants us to step out of our comfort zone and live in His glory zone. He wants us to take risks. He wants us not to shrink back and try to fit in with the crowd. He wants us not to live in fear. He wants us not to withhold giving to the kingdom because we fear what might happen tomorrow. No, God wants us to trust Him. Give big; love big!

Day 21

SEEK HIS RIGHTEOUSNESS

But seek first His kingdom and His righteousness, *and all these things will be added to you.*
—MATTHEW 6:33, EMPHASIS ADDED

THE MEANING OF this verse seems clear: if we seek the Lord first, He is going to bring other good things into our lives. But what does it mean to seek first God's kingdom and His *righteousness*?

When we hear the word *righteousness*, we often think about being a moral, trustworthy, and just person. This is a correct way to understand the term, but there is more to it. Being righteous is most fundamentally a matter of being rightly aligned with God. It is to live in harmony with Him, have our hearts reflect His heart, and think as He thinks.

When we get closer to Him by becoming more like Him, we experience His presence and fellowship in a more intimate and satisfying way. We begin to drink of His Spirit, and the deepest desires of our hearts slowly are fulfilled as we discover how close Yeshua is to us, who He is to us, and who we are to Him. As we seek Him first simply because we want to know Him, love Him, and please Him, He responds by adding so many other blessings to our lives.

The things that He adds to our lives are not the goal; they're the icing on the cake. He Himself is our reward. As the Lord said to Abraham, so He says to us today, "I am thy shield, and thy exceeding great reward."[1]

BOAST IN THE LORD

My soul will make its boast in the LORD;
the humble will hear it and rejoice.
—PSALM 34:2

DAVID'S CONFIDENCE IN the Lord was apparent to all. The mighty king of Israel wanted everyone to know about God's glory and his love for Yahweh. When we have the right spirit, it is good to boast in the Lord because others will see our conviction in Him and receive hope.

Sometimes we are so concerned about being humble that we don't convey the assurance we have in God, and the enemy uses this against us. At times, because we are afraid of being proud, we don't receive the certainty from the Lord that He wants us to have.

David said, "The humble will hear it and rejoice"! Why would the humble rejoice when David boasts in the Lord? It's because they were empowered by David's conviction. By boasting in the Lord, David radiated a light that lifted others and inspired them to trust God for themselves. Our surety can give others hope that they can be confident too.

Beloved one, if you know people who are oppressed or beaten up by life, when you humbly declare your confidence in the Lord, you minister confidence in the love of Yeshua to them. And your positivity can change their lives. So let us be like David and make our boast in the Lord. May the humble hear of our love for Messiah Jesus and as a result find hope for their own lives.

YOU WILL NOT BE PUT TO SHAME

*They looked to Him and were radiant, and
their faces will never be ashamed.*
—PSALM 34:5, EMPHASIS ADDED

THE "THEY" DAVID is referring to in today's verse is
you and me—God's elect children, whom He chose
to be His own even before the foundation of the world.[1]
We are destined to be radiant, and our faces will ulti-
mately never be ashamed.

Of course, that doesn't mean we won't have battles
to fight. As long as we are in this world, the powers
of darkness will resist us. In fact, Yeshua talked about
overcoming seven times in Revelation 2 and 3. In one
example, Yeshua said, "He who overcomes, I will grant
to him to sit down with Me on My throne, as I also
overcame and sat down with My Father on His throne."[2]

Overcoming requires action, determination, and a
focus on Yeshua and Father God. But as we keep our
eyes on Him, He will lead us to victory, and we will
become radiant. We will emanate a light that will be
obvious to all who see us.

Beloved one, we will not be put to shame. We are
more than conquerors in Yeshua! The Lord says, "Kings
will be your guardians, and their princesses your nurses.
They will bow down to you with their faces to the earth
and lick the dust of your feet; and you will know that I
am the LORD; those who hopefully wait for Me will not
be put to shame."[3]

Day 24

DISCERN THE SEASON YOU'RE IN

The Lord will fight for you while you keep silent.
—Exodus 14:14

THE MINISTRY OF God in our lives is like a multifaceted diamond. He is applying the ministry of the Holy Spirit to our lives in different ways during different seasons.

For example, in 1 Chronicles 14, after David defeated the Philistines, he said, "God has broken through my enemies *by my hand*, like the breakthrough of waters."[1] In other words, David was involved in winning the victory. But in today's verse, we see another facet of the Lord's activity. Father God told Israel to *stand still, keep silent, and just watch* what He alone was going to do.

There are times when God is asking us to step out, get busy, and take action. And there are other times when the Lord is telling us to be still and watch Him move. The Bible says, "To everything there is a season, and a time to every purpose under heaven."[2] Do you know what season you are in right now? Is this a season when the Holy Spirit is prompting you to stand up, take action, and not be passive? Or is it a season when the Lord is telling you to stop striving, be still, and know that He is God?

Beloved one, God is calling us to abide in Him. That may mean taking action or standing still. We must learn to discern the inner workings of the Holy Spirit as well as the season we're in.

CHOOSE TO BE THANKFUL

Every good thing given and every perfect gift is from
above, coming down from the Father of lights, with
whom there is no variation or shifting shadow.
—JAMES 1:17

D O YOU RECOGNIZE the many blessings Father God has given you? Let's think for a minute about the good things God has brought into our lives. Are you alive? Can you think? Do you love and receive love? Do you see God's beauty in His creation—the sky, the sun, the trees, and so on? Do you have family or friends whom you enjoy spending time with? Can you hear, touch, taste, or smell? Most importantly, do you know Yeshua and have the hope of spending eternity in heaven?

Everything that adds to our joy is a gift from God. Beloved one, Father is truly good, He is worthy to be praised, and He wants us to walk with an attitude of thanksgiving. In Luke 17, Yeshua told a story about ten lepers. He healed ten, but only one returned and thanked Him. Jesus asked, "Were there not ten cleansed? But the nine—where are they?"[1]

Unfortunately, this is the mindset of many believers today. Few of us are thanking Father God for all the good He has brought into our lives. If we want to experience more of God's goodness, we need to acknowledge what He has already done. This is a decision. We must choose to be thankful.

HE WILL COMPLETE THE WORK

For I am confident of this very thing, that He who began a good work in you will perfect it until the day of Christ Jesus.
—PHILIPPIANS 1:6

W<small>E ARE NOT</small> the ones who began God's work in our lives, and we are not the ones who are going to finish it. God is. What an incredible promise! This is why the writer of Hebrews says Jesus is "the author and perfecter of faith."[1] He began it, and He is going to finish it!

In the beginning of our faith walk, we know that the Lord is the One who saved us, but somehow along the way we start thinking that we have to perfect ourselves by our own good works. But Paul said, "He saved us, not on the basis of deeds which we have done in righteousness, but according to His mercy, by the washing of regeneration and renewing by the Holy Spirit."[2] In other words, don't substitute your faith for works because you weren't saved by works. You are saved because God has been merciful to you, and He will perfect the work He began in you.

Paul also said, "For by grace you have been saved through faith; and that not of yourselves."[3] I know there are times when we feel weak and doubt our own faith, but the Bible says when we are faithless, He remains faithful.[4] God is faithful, beloved one. He that began the good work in you will complete it.

Day 27

HE KNOWS YOU

O LORD, You have searched me and known me....Even before
there is a word on my tongue, behold, O LORD, You know it
all. You have enclosed me behind and before, and laid Your
hand upon me. Such knowledge is too wonderful for me.
—PSALM 139:1, 4–6

GOD KNOWS EVERY thought that comes to our mind. He knows every impulse of our personality. He sees us right where we are, and He's intimately acquainted with all our ways.

Take that in for a moment, beloved one. God is closer than close to you, and He knows you better than you know yourself. If you're married, God knows you better than your spouse because He knows your thoughts, even if you don't speak them. To say it another way, before you say a word, He knows exactly what you're thinking and what you're going to say. Only God truly knows you.

Notice what David says next: "You have enclosed me behind and before." Our lives are completely sealed in the Holy Spirit. In Yeshua, we are enclosed all around. Despite the wrong things we think and say, His hand is upon us. Just as David said, so too we say, "Such knowledge is too wonderful for me"!

Meditating on this invisible reality can make us feel extreme security. The words David spoke, "You have enclosed me," remind me of Paul's words to us in Ephesians 1:13, "You were sealed in Him with the Holy Spirit." May you and I fully grasp this revelation.

AN INDISPUTABLE REALITY

In the seventh month on the first of the month you shall have
a rest, a reminder by blowing of trumpets, a holy convocation.
—LEVITICUS 23:24

THE FEAST OF Trumpets is a solemn reminder of the day when the children of Israel gathered at the base of Mount Sinai, and the holy God of Israel manifested His presence atop the mountain. The fact that the Jewish people have been celebrating this every year for over thirty-five hundred years attests to the reality that it did, in fact, happen. It is a historical reality.

In a similar way, Messiah's return will be announced by the sound of a trumpet from heaven, and all humanity will witness it.[1] Yeshua's imminent return is a certainty, and Father God wants us to live in anticipation of it. This is the bedrock of our faith and why Jesus' last words in the Book of Revelation are, "Yes, I am coming quickly."[2] Let's keep our eyes focused on His return and each day live in the light of eternity.

Beloved one, Jesus is truly coming back for us, and He will reward each of us according to what we have done.[3] One day soon, there will be no more sorrow, pain, sickness, or heartache, but only eternal joy. We have this and more waiting for us. Yeshua is coming, and we will be with Him forever "in a moment, in the twinkling of an eye, at the last trumpet."[4]

WALK ON WATER

And He said, "Come!" And Peter got out of
the boat, and walked on the water.
—MATTHEW 14:29

YOU MAY BE familiar with the story of Peter walking on water. In this account, when Jesus told him to come, Peter stepped out of the boat and, keeping his eyes on Yeshua, did what was humanly impossible. But then Peter began to feel the wind blowing and saw the waves raging, which he allowed to take his focus off Messiah Yeshua. As a result, he began to sink.

Many of us in this age will probably never physically walk on water, but we can do the spiritual equivalent, which is to live above our circumstances. When Peter focused on Yeshua, he was able to live above the threat of the winds and the waves. It was only when he allowed the circumstances into his mind and heart that he became overwhelmed and sank. Every day, you and I are in a similar battle. Yeshua is saying to us, "Come. Keep your head up and your eyes and heart fixed on Me, and you will overcome every obstacle."

When we face relationship struggles, problems at work, battles with our health, and so many other issues on this side of glory, we can experience supernatural victory and avoid sinking as we stay focused on God, His Word, and His Spirit in the midst of the winds and waves of life. You too like Peter will walk on water in this world as you stay in faith and keep your eyes on Him.

Day 30

HE IS FULL OF COMPASSION

...who crowns you with lovingkindness and compassion.
—PSALM 103:4

GOD'S COMPASSION TOWARD us is boundless. Through Jesus, HaShem is able to sympathize with our weaknesses, and He desires to help us overcome our insecurities, fears, and doubts. This is something to be thankful for. God does not have to be compassionate and merciful. He could have responded to our sinfulness by wiping out mankind as He did during Noah's day.[1] But instead He has chosen, through the blood of Yeshua, to extend His love to us wholeheartedly.

Because of God's deep compassion for us, we can tell Him anything, including our struggles. We can open our lives to Him, knowing His response is always going to be filled with love. This doesn't mean He won't discipline us when necessary. He will. But we can be sure He is going to help us, as Yeshua did when He walked the earth: "Seeing the people, He felt compassion for them, because they were distressed and dispirited like sheep without a shepherd."[2]

I love what David said in Psalm 103: "Just as a father has compassion on his children, so the LORD has compassion on those who fear Him. For...He is mindful that we are but dust."[3] We must humble ourselves to receive God's compassion. Some of us are being harder on ourselves than He is toward us.

Beloved one, Father God adores you. He is full of compassion for you. Open your heart to Him.

Day 31

REFUSE TO BE STOPPED

When the Philistines heard that they had anointed David
king over Israel, all the Philistines went up to seek out David.
—2 SAMUEL 5:17

WHEN THE PHILISTINES heard David had been anointed king, they immediately rose up against him. The anointing on David's life made him a target to his enemy. Likewise, when we are walking deeper in the Spirit and operating in a greater anointing, the powers of darkness are going to respond to us. Why? Because we become more of a threat to their kingdom. Supernatural people attract opposition.

I experienced this firsthand several years ago. After reading in Hebrews 11:6 that the Lord is a rewarder of those who diligently seek Him, I decided to spend a day seeking God, believing He was going to reward me. I spent about twelve hours reading the Bible, praying, and listening to worship music.

That night after I went to bed, I was attacked by the most violent evil spirit I had ever encountered. The next morning, the enemy tempted me with the thought, "This is what happens when you pursue God; you'd better not seek Him anymore."

Obviously, the devil was trying to keep me from advancing in God by scaring me. Beloved one, when we are progressing in the Spirit, we are going to face resistance from the forces of evil, but by the grace of God, we must never let the enemy win. We must remain steadfast, keep pressing forward, and refuse to be stopped!

LISTEN TO THE SPIRIT

*For all who are being led by the Spirit
of God, these are sons of God.*
—ROMANS 8:14

IT TOOK ME a long time to start minding the checks from Father. The Holy Spirit would be giving me a subtle witness in my spirit, telling me, "No, don't do that." But I wouldn't pay attention. I would just do it anyway. Eventually I realized this was hurting me and, more importantly, hurting Father. And slowly over time, I learned to pay attention to those subtle checks of the Holy Spirit.

Perhaps you're the same way. Maybe God is checking you about certain things in your life—a relationship, your words, your diet, your attitude, or a financial decision—but you're not paying attention, so you keep finding yourself surrounded by chaos. Being led by God's Spirit is a matter of learning to heed the checks of the Holy Spirit and discern when the peace of God is nudging you to go forward.

Beloved one, the Holy Spirit is a real person you can experience right here and now. And He is speaking to you and bearing witness with your heart. If you will make it your ambition to stop walking in your own self-will and open your ears to Him, you will learn to walk by the Spirit. Father desires to be involved in all the decisions you make. If you desire to live under the direction of the Lord, listen like never before to the gentle voice of the Spirit and consider Him in everything you do.

RISE TO THE LEVEL OF FAITH

*I have fought the good fight, I have fin-
ished the course, I have kept the faith.*
—2 TIMOTHY 4:7

T HE "GOOD FIGHT" Paul speaks of is the war of faith.
Every day, we can either respond to life's challenges
in faith, or in fear and doubt. The choice is ours. We
must warfare to rise to the level of faith by reminding
ourselves of God's goodness and the integrity of His
Word. We must not yield to the powerful forces of darkness, disregarding the promises of the Scriptures. If we
do, we will find ourselves in a state of doubt and confusion, leading to depression and destruction.

So our challenge is to approach every day waging the
good fight of faith. You see, every time I'm faced with a
problem, I can either panic, complain, and speak words
of bitterness, or I can say, "Thank You, Father God, for
using everything in my life to bring me to the next level
in You. Thank You for this difficulty." James and Peter
taught us that we should rejoice when we encounter various trials because the hardships test our faith, meaning
they bring us into a state of maturity and wholeness.

Today, beloved one, let's choose to align ourselves
with the Lord and the truth of His Word. We can do
all things through Christ who strengthens us.[1] We will
be victorious in the face of our trials when we arm ourselves with God's Word and confidence in Yeshua's
goodness.

Day 34

TO BECOME LIKE HIM

But we all, with unveiled face, beholding as in a mirror
the glory of the Lord, are being transformed into the same
image from glory to glory, just as from the Lord, the Spirit.
—2 Corinthians 3:18

IF WE WANT to know God and walk in unity with Him, we have to clothe ourselves in His nature. This means we must control the desires of the flesh and instead take on the substance and attributes of God.

We must have *kavanah*, or intention, to restrict the inclinations of our carnal nature and adorn ourselves with humility, gentleness, love, peace, patience, goodness, self-control, and the other traits of the Spirit. The more we harness the flesh, the more we will be able to abide in the Spirit. Of course, it takes effort, strength, and *kavanah* to hold back our natural impulses. But if you will engage in warfare by constraining your flesh and choosing the higher ways of the Father, you will ascend in the power of the Spirit and enter into a relationship with God that is beyond anything you have ever known!

Beloved one, the more we restrain our flesh and clothe ourselves with the Spirit, the more like Jesus we will become. This requires discipline and a dying to self, but in the end we will be transformed into Yeshua's likeness. That prize is worth the sacrifice. Messiah said, "He who has found his life will lose it, and he who has lost his life for My sake will find it."[1]

THE LAST LAUGH

Jesus said, "I will make them come and bow down before your feet, and make them know that I have loved you."
—REVELATION 3:9

YESHUA PROMISED THAT as we cling to Him and make Him the Lord of our lives, He will cause us to reign over our enemies—over all those who have accused us, every spirit that has condemned us, and everyone who has mocked us! God is going to bring our lives to a triumphant conclusion, but until then we must continue to hold on and stay strong.

Nothing past, present, or future is capable of keeping God from fulfilling His word. Paul said God is "able to do far more abundantly beyond all that we ask or think."[1] We have to filter everything through the reality that God is limitless, invincible, and in control.

It looked like Yeshua had lost when He was on the cross. The soldiers mocked and spit on Him. They thrust a spear in His side and placed a crown of thorns on His head. It must have seemed like they had the last laugh. But God was not done. Messiah Jesus rose from the dead!

Beloved one, at times the enemy may seem to be winning, but stand your ground. Victory is assured! Your accuser, the devil, will have his day in "court" and receive the final judgment for all his false accusations.[2] So hold on and stay strong. You and I will have the last laugh.

BLESS THE LORD AT ALL TIMES

I will bless the LORD at all times; His praise
shall continually be in my mouth.
—PSALM 34:1

DAVID RESOLVED TO praise his God "continually." He awoke each morning with prayer and praise: "In the morning, O LORD, You will hear my voice; in the morning I will order my prayer to You and eagerly watch."[1]

I love that the priests of Israel were commanded to praise God every morning *and* evening: "They are to stand every morning to thank and to praise the LORD, and likewise at evening."[2] Our praise and prayer are to be perpetual, which means we must be bold enough to say, "Praise God," in public. Through our praise, we become lights revealing Father to the world.

I realize there is a time and place for everything, but too often we aren't conveying God's praise to the world as we should. Beloved one, don't let anyone keep you from acknowledging your Creator! David didn't compartmentalize his life so that he only praised God in specific places or at certain times. All David's talk was seasoned with praise to HaShem.

Likewise, we need to love God so much that we don't hesitate to speak of His goodness. May His praise be continually in our mouths, for we "are a chosen race, a royal priesthood...a people for God's own possession, so that [we] may proclaim the excellencies of Him who has called [us] out of darkness into His marvelous light."[3]

Day 37

WALK IN DIVINE HEALING

*But if the Spirit of Him who raised Jesus from the
dead dwells in you, He who raised Christ Jesus
from the dead will also give life to your mortal
bodies through His Spirit who dwells in you.*
—ROMANS 8:11

THIS VERSE IS so rich. Those of us who have been born again literally have the Spirit that raised Yeshua from the dead living in us. I hope you can truly grasp this reality. The Spirit that lifted Yeshua off the ground and caused Him to ascend and disappear into the clouds lives in you and me. We have resurrected, victorious life living inside us, and as we cling to Father God, He will teach us to live by this Spirit.

But that's not all. His Spirit imparts divine life that will keep our natural bodies healthy. That means if you and I feel like our bodies are getting sick or worn out, we can entreat God's Spirit who lives inside us to impart life and healing to our flesh so we can supernaturally recover and walk in divine health. As God's dear children, we can rely on His Spirit to give life to our mortal flesh so we can be in good health—body, soul, mind, and spirit—while we're on the earth.

Beloved one, God is so great, and in Messiah Yeshua we are complete.[1] Let's believe God to be for us who He said He would be—the source of our shalom, victory, and healing.

THE GOD OF COMFORT

*...if indeed we suffer with Him so that we
may also be glorified with Him.*
—ROMANS 8:17

NOT LONG AGO I awoke early one morning after dreaming about a painful encounter I had with some family members. The situation made me feel like an outsider to my own relatives, and in this dream I was reliving that episode and all the rejection and humiliation associated with it. I had been praying about the situation for close to two years, so when I woke up feeling the sting of the experience, I was unsettled and wondering why I was still dealing with the hurt.

Knowing I wouldn't be able to get back to sleep, I went to my prayer room and started talking to the Lord: "Father God, why am I still dealing with this pain? Help me through this. Let me know there's victory on the other side." Later that day, a friend texted me Romans 8:17, which tells us that we've been called to suffer with Christ and be glorified with Him. As I read the verse, I knew God was right with me in my pain, and I felt Him assuring me, "You're suffering because of Me, and You're going to receive My reward for it."

God is faithful. As He strengthened me during my moment of pain, so He will do for you. And in the end, you'll be glorified in the One who was raised from the dead and crowned King.

Day 39

THE FATHER IS THE DESTINATION

Blessed be the God and Father of our Lord Jesus
Christ, who has blessed us with every spiritual
blessing in the heavenly places in Christ Jesus.
—EPHESIANS 1:3, EMPHASIS ADDED

NOTE WHERE THE blessing is coming from. Paul says, "Blessed be the *God and Father* of our Lord Jesus Christ." What am I pointing out? Many Christians make Jesus the end of everything. They pray to Jesus. They sing to Jesus. They preach about Jesus. And obviously, we should. But the problem is they have left out God the Father. Yet Yeshua said, "Pray, then, in this way: '*Our Father* who is in heaven.'"[1] Jesus was always living unto the Father.

Oftentimes our walk is only focused on Jesus. But Jesus is not the end. The Father is the end. Jesus is the way, but the Father is the destination. Some of us have made the way the destination, but the way is the path *to* the destination, who is the Father.

Please don't misunderstand. I believe that Jesus is God in the flesh, that the Father was in Jesus and Jesus is in the Father. But Jesus came to bring us to the Father. This is why Yeshua said, "No one comes to the Father but through Me."[2] So if you find yourself always praying to Jesus, recognize that something is off in your heart's understanding of the Godhead. Remember, beloved one, it all comes from the Father—"for from Him and through Him and to Him are all things."[3]

135

THE GIFT OF OBSTACLES

*To the one who overcomes, I will grant to eat from
the tree of life, which is in the Paradise of God.*
—REVELATION 2:7

HAVE YOU EVER wondered why a compassionate God doesn't quickly remove all our problems, or why He let Adam and Eve fall in the first place? After all, the difficulties we experience are a result of the fall. If God cares so much, why didn't He prevent Adam and Eve from sinning? If He knew they were going to disobey Him, why didn't He take a different course? Beloved one, it may be hard to hear, but God uses evil so that we can be strengthened and made complete by overcoming it.

We actually grow by overcoming difficult things in our lives; this is part of God's plan. With each victory, we are transformed into who God wants us to be. "For momentary, light affliction is producing for us an eternal weight of glory far beyond all comparison."[1] Every obstacle becomes a stepping stone that leads us to our ultimate place in Him, which is being conformed to the image of Christ!

We cannot confuse our temporary reality, which involves discomfort, struggle, and pain, with the ultimate reality that God loves us and has a perfect plan for our lives. Our present challenges are the starting point from which we cultivate a deeper sense of who God is. All our obstacles are God's gift to us. They create the opportunity to overcome and be made complete in Him.

Day 41

OPEN YOUR HEART TO FAITH

*Therefore I say to you, all things for which you
pray and ask, believe that you have received
them, and they will be granted you.*
—MARK 11:24

YEARS AGO WHEN I was a teenager, I went to see *The
Exorcist*. It was such a traumatic experience. I knew
they couldn't have made a movie like that if evil and
demonic powers weren't real. That film made me so
afraid of being possessed by the devil that I would sneak
into my parents' room after they had fallen asleep and
sleep on the side of their bed. I felt like Satan was right
beside me. Fear gave the evil one access into my life.

I praise God that when I came to faith in Yeshua,
that fear instantly left me. You see, even as fear opens
a channel for the demonic, so too faith opens a channel
for God's courage to manifest in our lives. In other
words, just as the devil operates through fear, so God
operates through the channel of faith.

Beloved one, I want to encourage you today to close
your heart to everything but faith and the love of God.
Guard your thoughts and words so fear and doubt can't
gain a foothold. Seize God's Word and don't let anything else in. Fight the fight of faith. As you reject the
thoughts of the enemy and say yes to God's Word and
Spirit, more and more of His power will be manifest in
your life.

Day 42

THE BELLS AND THE POMEGRANATES

*But you will receive power when the Holy Spirit has
come upon you; and you shall be My witnesses.*
—ACTS 1:8

BEING AN AUTHENTIC witness is to represent Yeshua
to anyone God has appointed us to influence so they
will have an opportunity to either accept or reject Him.

This involves both our words and our deeds. The
ancient high priest of Israel wore a robe that had pomegranates and bells all around its hem: "A golden bell and
a pomegranate, all around on the hem of the robe. It
shall be on Aaron when he ministers."[1] The bells could
be heard; they represent our words that point people to
the Messiah. The pomegranates represent the fruit of
the Spirit, which should be reflected in our character
and the way we live our lives.

Too often Christians are extreme on one side of this equa-
tion. For example, some believers are very kind, thoughtful,
and giving, but they never tell those they're helping about
Jesus. This is like the high priest having pomegranates with
no bells. On the other hand, some of us may be very bold
in quoting the Bible to others, but we do it without sensitivity to the Spirit so that our witness comes off as hard and
uncaring because we lack compassion and love.

So the point, my beloved friend, is that we need both.
We need to influence others for Jesus by our words and
by the fruit of the Spirit that emanates from our personality and actions.

YOU CANNOT BE DEFEATED!

*But You, LORD, are a shield around me, my
glory, and the One who lifts my head.*
—PSALM 3:3

NO MATTER WHAT we are going through, we need to take our eyes off the situation and look instead to King Jesus, who ascended and sits at the Father's right hand in heaven. When we choose to look beyond our natural circumstances and fix our gaze upon the eternal God who created us, we will be transformed from glory to glory. All the events of our lives, good and bad, will be used to change us into His likeness.

We cannot be defeated! If we stay faithful and committed, looking to Messiah, He will cause us to ascend over all our difficulties. We will overcome every trouble and trial. Whatever we face, whether "tribulation, or distress, or persecution, or famine, or nakedness, or peril, or sword...in all these things we overwhelmingly conquer through Him who loved us."[1]

Beloved one, you are a winner, and your victory is assured. Dedicate your entire life to Messiah Jesus. Keep studying His Word and talking to Him. Keep surrounding yourself with other believers who enrich your faith. Discard anything that could distract, deter, or dissuade you from the truth. Avoid things that create opportunities for the enemy to speak to you and overwhelm you. If you continue to praise God, declaring that you are victorious in Messiah Jesus, you will continually find yourself triumphing over every situation.

Day 44

A HEAVENLY MINDSET

*Set your minds on the things that are above,
not on the things that are on earth.*
—COLOSSIANS 3:2

AS BELIEVERS IN Yeshua, we must live for the *age
to come*. We cannot allow our temporal circumstances or how people treat us to define who we are in
God or distract us from having a heavenly perspective.
We must set our focus on eternity even in the midst of
tests and trials.

We must keep our eyes on the eternal prize. This
world is not our home. Like Abraham, we are called
to set our sights on the majestic city "whose architect
and builder is God."[1] We must continually look toward
heaven. All our thoughts and actions should be filtered
through an eternal mindset.

Beloved one, we are not of this world, and it can never
satisfy us. Let us stop trying to gratify ourselves with
the fleeting pleasures of this life and instead live each
day realizing that we are on a supernatural journey.
Eternal life is our calling, and heaven is our destination.

As we age, we see more and more how temporary
our earthly life is. Many of us have family and friends
who have already passed away. So let's live for what will
endure. Soon Messiah will return, and for those who
have lived for Him, our final home will be in a place
where God will wipe every tear from our eyes and there
will no longer be any suffering, pain, or death.[2]

Day 45

WALK IN THE LIGHT

*But if we walk in the Light as He Himself is in the
Light, we have fellowship with one another, and the
blood of Jesus His Son cleanses us from all sin.*
—1 JOHN 1:7

To walk in the Light is to constantly reach out to
Jesus. As we follow Yeshua, the Light of the world,
we will be cleansed of our sin through His blood, the
living Word, and the Spirit. As a result, we will find
ourselves being brought into deeper and deeper communion with God.

It's the concept of similarity and dissimilarity at work.
Consider, for example, an elephant and a mouse. They
have nothing in common. They are dissimilar and have
no relational connection. But an elephant and another
elephant can be in relationship because they're alike. In
fact, elephant mothers train their young to survive.

Similarly, as we reach out to Jesus and He cleanses
us of sin, we are being transformed into His image and
actually become His friends. Yeshua said, "No longer do
I call you slaves...but I have called you friends."[1] The
more we become like Jesus, the closer we will feel to
Him and the more satisfying our relationship with God
will be. It is not enough just to know God in heaven;
we must also know Him from within. As we are transformed into His likeness, we experience unity with the
One who is the treasure of life and the fountain of many
waters.

Day 46

THE LAMB OF GOD

Seeing Yeshua approaching, John the Baptist
declared, "Behold, the Lamb of God who
takes away the sin of the world."
—JOHN 1:29

WHEN JOHN THE Baptist referred to Jesus as the Lamb of God, he was pointing back to the first Passover when the children of Israel were delivered out of Egypt through the blood of a lamb. Through divine revelation, John understood that Yeshua would become the final and ultimate sacrificial Lamb for all mankind.

Yeshua's last supper with His disciples before going to the cross was a Passover meal, where He foretold that He would die for us, ushering in a new covenant in His blood.[1] It was no coincidence that Yeshua was crucified on Passover. God preordained this to declare to the world that Yeshua's sacred blood fulfilled the ancient Passover miracle.

But consider this: it was not enough for the ancient Israelites to simply collect the lambs' blood in basins. They had to personally apply it to the doorposts of their homes. Likewise, it is not enough just to know Messiah shed His blood and died for our sins. We must personally receive Him into our hearts and follow Him so that His blood will be applied to our individual lives.

Beloved one, although Yeshua died two thousand years ago, His blood is yet alive, bringing salvation and deliverance to all who commit their lives to Him. When we are fully committed to Him, His blood covers our lives.

SET APART

*Paul, a bond-servant of Christ Jesus, called as
an apostle, set apart for the gospel of God.*
—ROMANS 1:1, EMPHASIS ADDED

EVEN AS PAUL was "set apart," so too as followers of
Yeshua, you and I are called to be separate. We are
to think and behave differently from the world around
us. In fact, Scripture says we are not of this world.[1]

We have been selected to live apart from this world
and to bring truth and the message of eternity to those
whom God brings into our lives. Of course, our words
will sometimes evoke a negative response. Think about
Paul. He was beaten, ridiculed, and maligned because
he was set apart. In fact, he wrote most of the New
Testament while in prison. Consider also the people of
Israel. They have been persecuted and hated from the
beginning of their history. We should expect the same,
and we must be willing to suffer the reproach of our
calling. "Indeed, all who desire to live godly in Christ
Jesus will be persecuted."[2]

Paul knew Yeshua in the power of His resurrection,
but he also knew what it meant to be rejected and feel
lonely because of his witness for Him. Beloved one, this
is also part of our call because we are set apart. But be
encouraged; you will be rewarded for all that you suffer
because of your love for Him! "Blessed are those who
have been persecuted for the sake of righteousness, for
theirs is the kingdom of heaven."[3]

LET HIM IN

True worshipers will worship the Father in spirit and truth.
—JOHN 4:23

HOW DO WE worship God in spirit and truth? It starts by being authentic. We have to be real. Many people get caught in a religious trap and only say prayers they learned from others. Although some memorized prayers can be powerful, to enter into deep waters in God, we need to bare our souls to the Lord. Father God wants us to confide in Him, sharing our deepest fears and desires.

We need to open our hearts to the Father because He can only come in to the degree we let Him. If our conversations with Him are limited to recited prayers, we are not disclosing who we really are, and He cannot dwell with us in a deep way. God already knows everything about us, so there is nothing to hide. Again, He can only come as far as we let Him.

This is a mystery in our relationship with God. Although the Father knows everything and is everywhere, He only dwells where He has an invitation. He is a gentleman. He can intrude anytime He wants, and He does do that at times. But that is not the kind of relationship the Lord wants. He is not looking for robots. He is looking for those who desire Him.

All creation is upheld by Messiah's power. But the only way we can be one with Him is if we choose to open our hearts and invite Him in.

LIFT YOUR HEAD

But God, being rich in mercy...raised us up with Him, and
seated us with Him in the heavenly places in Christ Jesus.
—EPHESIANS 2:4, 6

YEARS AGO BEFORE I was a believer, I went through a very difficult time. Although I was short growing up, I thought I would have a growth spurt and become tall like my cousins. But while in my late teens, I realized that wasn't going to happen. I was stuck at five-five-and-a-half.

Because I didn't know the Lord, this was a death blow to me. My spirit was crushed until I came to know Yeshua. Then I read that I was seated with Christ in heavenly places, and thought, "How much taller can I get than that?" I share this because many of us have been broken by life. We feel defeated by a spirit of inferiority, perhaps because of our income, our physical appearance, or things we were told growing up. But I want to remind you that you are a new creation and have been brought into supernatural unity with God through the blood of Yeshua. Now in the realm of the spirit, you are seated with Him in heavenly places. This means you're above everything and are a permanent victor in God.

Beloved one, you are somebody. You're not defined by your job, your stature, or what people say. What defines you is who God says you are, and He says you're a champion in Him. You're a winner. Lift your head and live like you believe Him!

PARTNERS IN LOVE

For the eyes of the LORD move to and fro
throughout the earth that He may strongly sup-
port those whose heart is completely His.
—2 CHRONICLES 16:9

HAVE YOU EVER thought about what makes human-kind different from God's other creations? First, we have a higher consciousness and, second, we have an ability to choose that is distinct from animal instincts. But what really makes us unique is that we were made in God's image, and He made us this way because He is looking for a partner in love.

God loves us, and He wants us to love Him back. But it would not be real love if God forced us to love Him. To have genuine relationship, we must consciously decide to love Him. We do this by being authentic with Him, disclosing our true selves, and by talking to Him more than we communicate with anyone else. We should be talking to God all the time—at work, at play, in the morning and evening. And we shouldn't limit our communication to what we say audibly. We can "talk" to HaShem simply by being conscious of Him. We can commune with Yeshua silently in the recesses of our soul.

Sometimes we think the problem is that God is too far away to hear us. But oftentimes the real problem is that we do not perceive how close He is. Beloved one, He is closer to us than our own heartbeat, but we must have faith to open our hearts and receive Him.

Day 51

EXPECT RESISTANCE

*Beloved, do not be surprised at the fiery ordeal
among you, which comes upon you for your testing, as
though some strange thing were happening to you.*
—1 PETER 4:12

I ONCE READ A true story about a man who for years
had known God was calling him into the ministry but
was reluctant to obey because he had a very secure job.
Finally, he decided to trust God and go into full-time
ministry, but before he announced his decision, the company offered him a big promotion. Why? The enemy was
trying to stop him from advancing in God's plan.

Beloved one, when we're following God, we will face
resistance. The battle we're in is not primarily against
flesh and blood; it's supernatural.[1] If we do not grasp
this, the enemy will thwart us in our pursuit of God.
We must anticipate spiritual opposition so we won't be
caught off guard when it comes.

When you trust God to surrender to Him in a deeper
way and are advancing in His call on your life, expect
to be opposed. Don't be astonished or dismayed when
you come under enemy fire. Consider Messiah Jesus.
Immediately after He was baptized in the Jordan River
and anointed by the Holy Spirit, the devil entered the
picture and tried to take Him off course.[2]

You and I will be resisted by the powers of darkness,
so let's remember what Messiah said: "Be faithful unto
death, and I will give you the crown of life."[3]

147

GUARD YOUR RELATIONSHIP
WITH YESHUA

*For you were continually straying like sheep, but now you
have returned to the Shepherd and Guardian of your souls.*
—1 PETER 2:25

SOME OF US can relate to this verse. We once were in
the world, doing things we knew were wrong. But
now we have returned to Jesus, the guardian of our
souls. Father God is challenging us today to not stray
again—to resist the temptation to compromise again
with the world.

Even though you love Jesus, you may find yourself
drawn toward things you shouldn't do and places you
shouldn't go. Don't play games with God. Don't meddle
with the world. Jesus has more for you. Yeshua said He
came to give us life and to give it more abundantly.[1] But
we can't receive the fullness of the blessing He wants to
give us until we separate ourselves unto Him.

Beloved one, Father has called us back to Himself.
Let's not put ourselves in relationships that will compromise our walk with Yeshua. Let's not put ourselves
in situations where we are tempted to engage in activi-
ties we were once addicted to. Let's guard our relationship with Messiah Jesus. Stay in the center of His heart.

Yeshua is the guardian of our souls. He has good
plans and a good future for us. Let's live in fidelity to
the Lord so that He can bless us and do what He wants
to do in our lives. "No good thing does He withhold
from those who walk uprightly."[2]

CHOOSE TO PRAISE THE LORD

Every day I will bless You, and I will
praise Your name forever and ever.
—PSALM 145:2

IF YOU'RE ANYTHING like me, some days you awake feeling refreshed, and other days you feel sluggish and unmotivated. On those days, you may not feel like praising God. But I want to encourage you to consciously choose to start your day by blessing the Lord, even when you don't feel like it, because this decision will affect the course of your day.

This is the law of firstfruits. Giving God the first part of our day orders the rest of it. When we decide to sit before the Lord first thing in the morning and thank Him for His goodness and declare His praise, suddenly our emotions change, and God begins to empower us. We may have had no desire to praise Him just five minutes earlier, but after electing to do so as an act of our will, we soon find ourselves feeling good. We have joy. Our perspective changes. Through transitioning ourselves in the spirit by choosing to put God first, we shifted the atmosphere.

Jesus did not say, "Whosoever feels, come." He said, "Whosoever will come after me, let him deny himself, and take up his cross, and follow me."[1] Beloved one, we can't control how we feel, but we can control our will. Let's choose to give God the firstfruits of our day and set our course in Him. The more you do this, the stronger, happier, and more stable you will be.

BE HOLY

But like the Holy One who called you, be holy
yourselves also in all your behavior.
—1 PETER 1:15

To be holy means to be set apart and unlike the world. It is to be peculiar and cut out from the rest. In other words, as children of the King, we are to look different, talk different, and be different.

One way I have chosen to show I am set apart is to grow out the side locks of my hair, which are called *peyot*. I know some people think this is a bit strange, but I believe I am called to be a *shaliach*, a sent-out one or messenger, of Yeshua in the earth. I have to be set apart to convincingly convey the unique ministry God has given me.

The same is true for you. I am not suggesting you grow *peyot* but that you live separate from the world and fully unto Jesus. By doing so, others will recognize that you are different, and God will use your uniqueness to draw people to Himself. Of course, this may cost you. Some may mock and reject you for being different and declaring your faith. But you are in good company. Yeshua was ridiculed and even crucified, but He overcame, and so will we!

Beloved one, let us make it a priority to submit ourselves as holy vessels unto God. We have been chosen to be set apart so that through our lives God's light will shine in the darkness.

Day 55

CREATED TO DO GOOD WORKS

*For we are His workmanship, created in Christ
Jesus for good works, which God prepared before-
hand so that we would walk in them.*
—EPHESIANS 2:10

IT'S IMPORTANT FOR us to realize that we are called to
serve in this world. God created us and is continuing
to form us to do good works and bear fruit. We're called
to make a difference and build God's kingdom in the
earth. We don't live under the Law or base our salvation
on our performance, but the fruit of being alive in the
Spirit is doing good works.

Today's verse goes on to tell us that the good works
we are called to walk in were actually prepared for us
in advance. For example, when you speak a word of
wisdom to someone, somehow that encounter and
relationship were actually prepared beforehand. God
ordained for you to cross paths so you could impart
into him or her what the Holy Spirit has sown in you. I
know that's a lot to get our heads wrapped around. But
we're dealing with the God of eternity here!

Beloved one, let's be cognizant today that God created
good works beforehand for us to walk in. Let's not miss
these opportunities. We will be rewarded for everything
we do in Yeshua's name, even things that seem insignifi-
cant like giving somebody a glass of water.[1] Scripture
encourages us to "be on the alert, stand firm in the
faith...be strong."[2] So let's stay awake and make the
most of each day.

151

DON'T BE PASSIVE

All the Philistines went up to seek out David; and when
David heard of it, he went down to the stronghold.
—2 SAMUEL 5:17

WHEN DAVID HEARD he was under attack, he didn't just passively sit there and let the enemy succeed. He went down to the stronghold and sought the Lord. He answered the attack aggressively by taking action.

Often when we are under attack, we do the opposite. We are passive and just let the enemy beat us up. Whether it is a mental or physical attack, too many of God's people put their heads in the sand and hope it just goes away. David didn't do that. He went to God's stronghold and looked to the Lord. He began to pray and encourage himself in the Word of God. He responded to the attack by digging down deep into the Lord, and his actions shifted the atmosphere and led the Israelites to victory.

Beloved one, God did not create us to be on the defense against the forces of darkness. He made us to be on the offense! Yeshua aggressively came against the forces of darkness. "The Son of God appeared for this purpose, to destroy the works of the devil."[1]

When the enemy has us under siege, we need to get in motion like David did, because motion will change our emotion. By doing something—adjusting our attitude, shifting our focus, going into prayer, and declaring God's Word—we will change the spiritual atmosphere around us and overcome!

FEAR THE LORD

The fear of the LORD is the beginning of wisdom.
—PROVERBS 9:10

THE CHURCH TODAY has glossed over the fear of the Lord. In fact, some are saying that God does not really want us to fear Him, only revere Him. Yes, we need to honor and respect Him, but I am going beyond just honoring and respecting God. We need a holy fear of the Lord. "The fear of the LORD is clean, enduring forever."[1] There is something clean and holy about fearing the Lord.

Fearing God puts us in proper alignment with Him, resulting in Father pouring His grace, mercy, and love upon us. Even Messiah Yeshua fears the Lord.[2] Demonic fear paralyzes, but the fear of the Lord brings us into freedom from the powers of darkness. To experience Father God in His fullness, we must both fear Him and embrace His loving-kindness.

Hear Jesus' words: "Do not fear those who kill the body but are unable to kill the soul; but rather fear Him who is able to destroy both soul and body in hell."[3]

Beloved one, one day we are going to be face-to-face with the eternal, self-existent God who has no beginning and no end. In that moment, we will certainly know exactly what it means to fear the Lord. Let us not wait until then to humble ourselves. Let us fear the Lord now. It truly is the beginning of wisdom and our relationship with God.

DRINK DEEPLY OF THE SPIRIT

*But whoever drinks of the water that I will give him shall
never thirst; but the water that I will give him will become
in him a well of water springing up to eternal life.*
—JOHN 4:14

MESSIAH JESUS IS the water that saturates our souls
and satisfies our deepest desires. But to experience this divine life, we must drink deeply of the Spirit.

Living a full Christian life takes more than being
immersed in Christian culture; we must enter the supernatural realm of the Spirit. This is an individual journey.
Just as God called Abraham to leave the familiar and
go into a new land, so is God calling us to leave what
we have known to follow His Spirit into something
greater—the realm of eternity.

Entering into the heavenly realm of eternal life is a
process. We must let God teach and train us to abide
in Him and hear His voice. We must learn to trust and
follow Him even when He's leading us to do things that
don't make sense to us or that stretch us out of our comfort zones. But as we obey Him as Abraham did, we will
enter a place in life that is full of light, fulfilling, and
beautiful.

This is why Yeshua said, "It is the spirit who gives
life."[1] As we keep drawing near to Him and from Him,
we will be transformed. And as time goes by, we will
become fuller, happier, and more content in Messiah
Jesus.

RENEWED LIKE THE EAGLE

Bless the LORD, O my soul...who satisfies your years with
good things, so that your youth is renewed like the eagle.
—PSALM 103:2, 5

I HAVE A FRIEND who is in her nineties and has known the Lord for more than fifty years. Every time I see her, it is like she just got saved. She always has a new joy or a fresh revelation. Although her hair is gray and she can hardly walk, she glows with a supernatural peace and youthfulness. When I see her, I feel I am witnessing the reality of God's Word in today's verse—Elohim will be the portion of those who put their trust in Him, renewing their youth even when their hairs are gray.

You may be getting older and experiencing new aches and pains and thinking, "My youth is not being renewed like the eagle," as David said. I understand, but listen, the Scripture says: "Though our outer man is decaying, yet our inner man is being renewed day by day."[1] We are not our hair, body, face, or even our vital organs. Who we truly are is who we are inside.

Beloved one, I have my hopes set on this: if we will seek God first, our later years will be our best years in the Spirit. The power of God will dwell more deeply in us and become stronger upon us. And even though our outer man is decaying, our inner man will rise up with the strength of an eagle.

TRANSFORMED BY OUR TRIALS

*For momentary, light affliction is producing for us an
eternal weight of glory far beyond all comparison.*
—2 CORINTHIANS 4:17

JESUS UNDERSTOOD THAT everything in His life had
a divine purpose. Even when He was facing evil
plots and schemes, Yeshua knew God had a reason
for allowing them, and He trusted the Father in every
situation.

When we face trials or circumstances we don't understand, it is easy to let doubt creep in and question God.
Some even get angry with Him. But Jesus' example was
to trust Father God's faithfulness and His heart, which
overflows with love and compassion for us. Our God is
good, but His thoughts are above our thoughts, and His
ways are above our ways.[1] We must trust Father even
when we do not fully comprehend His purpose.

I know this is easier said than done. Because we see
what is in the temporal realm, we often draw conclu-
sions based on what we perceive in the natural, not
realizing the bigger picture and that so much more is
happening in the spirit. God has an eternal plan that
is bigger than we know. When we go through earthly
trials loving God and staying faithful and obedient to
Him, our challenges will work to our benefit. This is
why James 1:2 tells us, "Consider it all joy, my brethren,
when you encounter various trials." Make no mistake,
beloved one: the temporary trials we face pale in comparison to the eternal weight of glory they work in us.

Day 61

KNOW GOD AND MAKE HIM KNOWN

But when He, the Spirit of truth, comes, He will
guide you into all the truth; for He will not speak on
His own initiative, but whatever He hears, He will
speak; and He will disclose to you what is to come.
—JOHN 16:13

THE HOLY SPIRIT is God's manifest presence to us. He will guide us into all truth and impart revelation. HaShem is in heaven, but the Spirit of God, the Ruach HaKodesh, is here on the earth to disclose Father to us and bring us closer to Him through Yeshua. The Holy Spirit will take of Jesus—His heart, nature, and will for our lives—and impart it to us.

God gave us the gift of His Spirit to empower us continually, abide in us, and make real His boundless love in our lives. The Spirit is our breath—our very life. Without the Spirit, we cannot truly know God or fully belong to Him. And through the Spirit, we are empowered to be bold witnesses.[1]

As God's Spirit enables us to know God, it is our responsibility to then make Him known. There are people all around us who do not know Jesus. "Therefore, we are ambassadors for Christ, as though God were making an appeal through us; we beg you on behalf of Christ, be reconciled to God."[2] As the Spirit of God brings us into a deeper experience with Messiah Jesus, let us also make Him known to others by being His witnesses.

GUARD AGAINST DISTRACTION

*Let your eyes look directly ahead and let
your gaze be fixed straight in front of you.*
—PROVERBS 4:25

KING DAVID'S SON Solomon had a supernatural weight of divine wisdom that was upon him so heavy that no one, before him or since, has ever been as wise. In today's verse, Solomon tells us something that is more important than it may seem upon first reading. He is not merely saying we need to keep our focus on what's in front of us; he is highlighting the extreme importance of guarding ourselves from distraction.

We are continually bombarded with distractions from the outer world, whether it's the internet, social media, television, or people calling or texting us. On top of that, we're being distracted by the enemy, who will use any means to get us off course, whether it's causing us to think about an ungodly thought that leads to death or stirring us to be fearful and anxious.

In order to guard our eyes, or focus, we need to create a conscious awareness of HaShem in our inner man. Ecclesiastes 2:14 says, "The wise man's eyes are in his head." In other words, a wise man is not constantly looking out in the world. A wise man is self-possessed. He is taken up with his internal dialogue with God. As a result of being focused on the Holy Spirit within him, he keeps his eyes in his own head.

Ask the Holy Spirit to teach you how to keep your eyes in your own head!

Day 63

AN ATTITUDE REALIGNMENT

I will praise the name of God with song and
magnify Him with thanksgiving.
—PSALM 69:30

HAVE YOU EVER wondered how two people raised in the same home, with the same parents, and near the same age can have completely different perspectives on life? This shows that our outlook is determined by more than just our circumstances. Our attitude can transcend our environment. With God's help, we can control our mindset.

You may know people who seem to have everything yet are bitter and depressed. Meanwhile, others who have very little materially radiate with joy. How do we explain the difference? The fact is, we choose our attitude, and it has far more power over our lives than any storm we may face. I know a man who grew up in tough circumstances. He does not have much money, and he has some significant challenges. But every time I ask him how he is, he says, "Better than I deserve." He is grateful and thankful just to be alive.

We have so much to be thankful for. If we will focus on what we have instead of what we lack, we will see the cup is half-full, not half-empty. Beloved one, we can walk in victory or defeat; our attitude is up to us. Father God has "set before you life and death, the blessing and the curse. So choose life in order that you may live."[1] Let us choose to be thankful and magnify the Lord, for this brings peace, joy, and life.

Day 64

A SPIRIT OF EXCELLENCE

Whoever speaks, is to do so as one who is speaking the utterances of God; whoever serves is to do so as one who is serving by the strength which God supplies; so that in all things God may be glorified through Jesus Christ.
—1 PETER 4:11

SOME PROFESSING CHRISTIANS wave their faith in front of them like a big flag, yet aren't committed to excellence in their lives and relationships. Beloved one, God is calling us to excellence. None of us is perfect, and I don't want anyone to feel shame or condemnation. But I do want to call us to a higher standard.

Peter said whoever speaks or serves should do so as one speaking for or serving Christ Jesus. Let's not use our Christianity as an excuse to not do our best. Some people think, "Oh, Jesus forgives," and then use that as an excuse to be lukewarm and spiritually lazy. God is a God of excellence, and He has given us the power by His Spirit to operate in a spirit of excellency and fruitfulness so Yeshua can be glorified in our lives.

He has called us "by His own glory and excellence."[1] Father's purpose is that people would look at believers and see something powerful, beautiful, special, and godly upon us and as a result they would look up to the Lord. I want to challenge you today to serve the Lord wholeheartedly. Let's give God our best. He deserves nothing less.

LORD WILLING

Come now, you who say, "Today or tomorrow we will go
to such and such a city, and spend a year there and engage
in business and make a profit." Yet you do not know what
your life will be like tomorrow....Instead, you ought to say,
"If the Lord wills, we will live and also do this or that."
—JAMES 4:13–15

BACK IN THE eighties when I was the captain of my church's softball team, we were playing a game one day and beating the opposing team by something like 16 to 1. I got cocky and jokingly said, "This game is over." You know what happened? We lost the game. And that taught me a deep lesson, not only about being humble but also about being careful with my words and not presuming anything.

This is what James is talking about in today's verse. It may seem strange to say "if the Lord wills," but the truth is, there are no guarantees. We don't know what's around the corner or even if we will be alive here on earth tomorrow. Beloved one, we need to humble ourselves and not be presumptuous. We need to say, "I'll be there tomorrow, Lord willing," or, "I'll do that tomorrow, Lord willing." Practicing this type of speech puts us in a posture of humility. And it's only in a posture of humility that Father God can draw us close to Himself. "God resisteth the proud, but giveth grace unto the humble."[1]

WALK BY FAITH

And without faith it is impossible to please Him, for
he who comes to God must believe that He is and
that He is a rewarder of those who seek Him.
—HEBREWS 11:6

THERE ARE TWO elements of faith: (1) believing that
God is and (2) that He is a rewarder of those who
diligently seek Him. It's that simple.

Some people think it's hard to believe in God, but the
beauty of God's creation alone is proof that He exists.
"Since the creation of the world His invisible attributes,
His eternal power and divine nature, have been clearly
seen, being understood through what has been made, so
that they are without excuse."[1] This means every one of
us, when we see creation, knows there is a God. And
because we know there is a God, we must surrender our
wills to Him. In other words, when we come to grips
with the reality that there is a Creator and that we are
His creation, we must turn and surrender to the One
who made us to fulfill His purpose for our lives.

We were made to seek after God and discover Him.
This is why we were born. The Lord said to Israel, "You
will seek Me and find Me when you search for Me with
all your heart."[2] Beloved one, I want to ask you today, is
your life at a place where you can say you are seeking
after God with all your heart?

Day 67

BUILD ON THE ROCK

*Everyone who hears these words of Mine and does
not act on them, will be like a foolish man who built
his house on the sand. The rain fell, and the floods
came, and the winds blew and slammed against
that house; and it fell—and great was its fall.*
—MATTHEW 7:26–27

EVERY ONE OF us sooner or later is going to experience challenges in life, whether it's a result of us getting older, losing a job, or having a health issue. How we handle the difficulties we face depends on the foundation our lives are built on. In Jesus' parable about the man who built his house on the sand, Yeshua is pointing out the disastrous end that awaits anyone who doesn't build their lives upon Him. They will be swept away, just as sand is washed away during a storm.

On the other hand, consider the outcome of the one who anchors their soul in God. "The righteous man will flourish like the palm tree, he will grow like a cedar in Lebanon. Planted in the house of the Lord, they will flourish in the courts of our God. They will still yield fruit in old age; they shall be full of sap and very green."[1]

Beloved one, I want to encourage you to make God the priority in your life. Spend time alone with Him *every day*. Let us truly live for the Lord and build our lives on the solid rock of Messiah Yeshua!

HUMBLE YOURSELF

Whoever exalts himself shall be humbled; and who-
ever humbles himself shall be exalted.
—MATTHEW 23:12

WHEN MESSIAH JESUS made His grand entrance into Jerusalem, He didn't embrace the pomp and circumstance expected of a king. Instead, Yeshua entered the Old City riding a donkey. The One who created the universe with His words chose to make His triumphal entry sitting humbly upon a donkey for all to see.

This gives us an incredible insight into the nature of God. Our great Father is gentle and humble of heart, and because of this we can actually move Him. When we voluntarily choose to love Him, it warms His heart. In fact, we can actually add to Father's happiness when we choose to please Him and put Him first. Consider that we can even make Him weep as Yeshua did after Lazarus died.[1] We can either move Father to joy or to tears. That is God's genius in creating you and me in His own image. Even though our God is complete and needs nothing, we can touch Him because He is so gentle and humble in heart.

The question is, Will we humble ourselves also? The Lord says, "But to this one I will look, to him who is humble and contrite of spirit."[2] Beloved one, let's choose to love Him with our whole heart by rejecting pride and choosing love. Yeshua said, "Whoever then humbles himself as this child, he is the greatest in the kingdom of heaven."[3]

Day 69

DEVELOPING SPIRITUAL DISCERNMENT

For you have not received a spirit of slavery leading to fear again, but you have received a spirit of adoption as sons by which we cry out, "Abba! Father!"
—ROMANS 8:15

As we grow in Christ, we will grow in spiritual discernment. "But solid food is for the mature, who because of practice have their senses trained to discern good and evil."[1] Too many of us think our thoughts are just thoughts. But today's verse says thoughts that produce fear are tied to a spirit.

As believers in Yeshua, we have not received a spirit of slavery leading to fear. Those thoughts that make you anxious are tied to a spirit, and you can reject them. And remember that you are not your thoughts. Having an anxious thought doesn't mean you are afraid. God has not given you a spirit of fear, but of love and power and a sound mind—a spirit of freedom.

As we grow in grace, we will recognize the thoughts that cripple us: thoughts that bring us down to operate in the realm of the flesh. They might be thoughts of anxiety, animosity, small-mindedness, fear, jealousy, accusation, and wanting to control. We have the authority to say no to those spirits. "No, I'm not going to receive that spirit. It has defeated me for too long, and I reject it today." As we learn to do that, we see God's truth, and we stay there.

Day 70

FRIENDS OF GOD

No longer do I call you slaves, for the slave does
not know what his master is doing; but I have
called you friends, for all things that I have heard
from My Father I have made known to you.
—JOHN 15:15

As you may know, the nation of Israel can be traced back to Abraham. And Genesis 22:18 says in Abraham's seed "all the nations of the earth shall be blessed." But what exactly does that mean for you and me today?

Galatians 3:14 tells us that the blessing of Abraham has come upon everyone who puts their faith in Messiah Jesus. So even if you are not Jewish by birth, if you have come into a relationship with the God of Israel through Yeshua, *the blessing of Abraham has come to you.* In light of that, consider this: in Isaiah 41:8 the Lord calls Abraham His friend. That means through Yeshua, you are also in friendship with God because you share in the blessing of Abraham. You have been "grafted in."[1] And "now in Christ Jesus you who previously were far away have been brought near by the blood of Christ."[2]

This should excite you, beloved one! God is not holding us at arm's length. He doesn't treat us like strangers or, worse, like enemies. When we put our trust in Yeshua, He brings us into His confidence and calls us His friends. Let's respond by talking to Him about everything and making Him our *best friend.*

FILL HIS HOUSE

*Go out into the highways and hedges, and compel
them to come in, that my house may be filled.*
—LUKE 14:23

WHETHER WE REALIZE it or not, many of the
people we encounter in life are hurting, have lost
hope, and need to know the Father's love for them. God
is looking for us to be His instruments to share the message of Yeshua with them.

Time is short! It is not enough for us to come together
and sing songs and recite Bible verses. We are the salt of
the earth and the light of the world. We have been given
a divine assignment to reach the world. We all have
work to do. You don't have to be on television or go to
the other side of the world. I like the phrase "Everyone
can reach someone."

I don't say this to condemn anyone. I say it to wake us
up. We need to step out of our comfort zones and accept
the call to share Jesus with others. Yeshua said, "As the
Father has sent Me, I also send you."[1] Will you say *yes*
to Jesus' assignment?

If you're serious about being an effective witness for
Yeshua, make it a priority. Ask Father God to place
people in your path who need His Son and will receive
your testimony. Ask Him to give you boldness, creativity,
and a fresh anointing to share your faith. As you choose
to love and obey, the Holy Spirit will anoint your words.

REPLACE IT WITH HIM

*Then Jesus said to His disciples, "If anyone
wishes to come after Me, he must deny himself, and take up his cross and follow Me."*
—MATTHEW 16:24

YESHUA SAID, "WHOEVER wishes to save his life will
lose it; but whoever loses his life for My sake will
find it. For what will it profit a man if he gains the
whole world and forfeits his soul? Or what will a man
give in exchange for his soul?"[1]

Too often, we are not wholly submitted to the Lord.
Many people are seeking an experience with God just to
make themselves feel good without actually becoming
true disciples and followers of Jesus. True anointing
comes from the Holy Spirit, who is given to those who
obey God.

The gospel calls us to surrender to God in obedience.
This is something we can do only by God's grace, but
we must choose to say *yes* to Him. Yeshua taught that
if we want to follow Him, we must be willing to give
up everything: our lives, our reputations, our material
things, and even our will. We need to stop depending
on and relying on anything other than God. This is the
point of Yeshua's words to the rich young ruler: "Go and
sell your possessions and give to the poor."[2]

Beloved one, there is a price to pay. We must pick
up our cross daily, lay our lives down, and follow Him.
There is no other way.

A REMEDY FOR FEAR

Immediately Jesus stretched out His hand and took hold of him, and said to him, "You of little faith, why did you doubt?" When they got into the boat, the wind stopped.
—MATTHEW 14:31–32

BELOVED ONE, IF you are struggling with fear or doubt, there is a remedy: have faith in God's Word. When Jesus told Peter to step out of the boat and walk on the water, Peter took God at His word and did something supernatural. But as soon as he took his focus off Yeshua and His word, Peter began to sink. When we stop believing God's Word, we start to sink too. But when we apply God's Word to our specific fears and anxieties, we will overcome them in the same way Peter overcame the laws of nature when he walked on water.

How do we do this? Find scriptures that combat your insecurities or doubts and keep those verses in front of you. Write them on index cards and put them in your car, on your bathroom mirror, at your desk at work, on the refrigerator—anywhere you will regularly see them. *Commit them to memory* and quote them every time that fear arises, declaring your victory by faith.

The Lord has destined us to be victorious in Messiah Jesus. But we must fight the good fight of faith by inviting Him into the deepest parts of our lives and using the sword of the Spirit, which is the Word of God.[1]

Day 74

LOOK UP

Therefore if you have been raised up with Christ, keep
seeking the things above, where Christ is, seated at the right
hand of God. Set your mind on the things above, not on the
things that are on earth. For you have died and your life is
hidden with Christ in God. When Christ, who is our life, is
revealed, then you also will be revealed with Him in glory.
—COLOSSIANS 3:1–4

YESHUA HAS BEEN raised from the dead and is seated
at the right hand of God in heaven. Paul tells us this
is where our focus needs to be. We need to be looking up,
seeking to be filled with the inheritance and resources
that are ours in Messiah Jesus.

As followers of Jesus, we've been severed from sin and
made alive in Christ. We've been raised up to walk in
newness of life, a life that's alive unto God. So we need
to draw our resources, shalom, joy, and identity from
heavenly places, not from the earth. And the Scripture
says if we do this, when the whole world sees Yeshua for
who He is, we will be revealed with Him in glory.

Beloved one, I want to encourage you today to deny
the lust of the flesh. Deny worldly ambitions. Let's not
draw from the natural realm but from the supernatural
realm. When we hunger and thirst after Jesus, we will
be filled. We will become lights in the darkness. And
when Messiah Jesus is finally revealed, we will be glorified with Him.

THE GIFT OF REVELATION

*Therefore I speak to them in parables; because
while seeing they do not see, and while hearing
they do not hear, nor do they understand.*
—MATTHEW 13:13

THIS VERSE PRESENTS a conundrum. It indicates that
Jesus not only revealed knowledge but that He also
concealed it. To those who drew near to Him for the
right reasons, He released revelation. But to those who
came to Him with pride and wrong motives, He concealed truth. Matthew 13 also says, "Whoever does not
have, even what he has shall be taken away from him."[1]
In other words, people who didn't receive His message
would lose even the little revelation they had been given.

This is a hard truth, but I share it to remind you that
when you know Jesus, you have been given a precious gift.
You don't know Yeshua because you're smarter than other
people or because you were born into the right home. If
you have revelation, it's because God has given it to you.
He has revealed to you what He has hidden from others.
This is why Messiah said in John 6:44 that no one comes
to Him unless the Father draws him. You look around and
see people who don't believe the way you do because they
have not been drawn and given the revelation you have.

Beloved one, you've been given a priceless gift.
Treasure it. Don't take it for granted. And while you're
here on the earth, share the light the Lord has given you
with others.

Day 76

FIRST PLACE

*"Teacher, which is the great commandment in the Law?" And
He said to him, "'You shall love the Lord your God with all
your heart, and with all your soul, and with all your mind.'"*
—MATTHEW 22:36–37

MANY PEOPLE THINK loving God means acknowledging Him, attending church services, or giving financially to build His kingdom. Those are all good things, but loving God is far more than that. It means to put God first and make Him Lord in every area of our lives.

There are some people who say they love God and do certain "Christian" things, but much of the time, they're not even thinking about Him. This isn't the fullness of the love that Father God is seeking. To love God with all our heart, soul, mind, and strength means there is no area we don't include Him in. All means all; anything less is unacceptable. Jesus said, "He who loves father or mother…son or daughter more than Me is not worthy of Me."[1] Messiah Jesus is either the Lord of all, or He's not our Lord at all.

Beloved one, we need to cultivate the Lordship of Yeshua—in our thoughts, our emotions, our actions— every day, all the time. Jesus will not be second best. He wants us to give Him our all. He loves us too much and is too holy to settle for anything else. If we truly love God with all our heart, we will have clarity in our lives.

UNWAVERING FAITH

Without becoming weak in faith he [Abraham] contem-
plated his own body, now as good as dead since he was about
a hundred years old, and the deadness of Sarah's womb;
yet, with respect to the promise of God, he did not waver
in unbelief but grew strong in faith, giving glory to God.
—ROMANS 4:19–20

IN GENESIS 18, the Lord appeared to Abraham and said, "I will surely return to you at this time next year; and behold, Sarah your wife will have a son."[1] As you may know, there was just one problem: Abraham and Sarah were well past the age of childbearing. In the natural, there was no hope of them conceiving a child. But Abraham believed in something bigger and more reliable than his circumstance. And he was rewarded for his faith with the birth of his son Isaac.

Sometimes what God has told us seems impossible, but faith will always believe God. We are to walk by faith and not by sight,[2] and we do this by clinging to God's Word. We agree with what we sense the Holy Spirit is speaking to our hearts, and we trust that what we are believing for will come to pass, even if we can't see how.

Beloved one, if you are praying for something that is according to God's Word, don't lose heart. Think about Abraham. Although his faith was tested, he never wavered. Don't allow the visible world to weaken your faith. Stay steadfast, and your day will come!

HE WILL MAKE IT RIGHT

*Assuredly, the evil man will not go unpunished, but
the descendants of the righteous will be delivered.*
—PROVERBS 11:21

SOMETIMES THINGS HAPPEN in life that just don't seem fair, and we're tempted to take vengeance on those we think treated us unjustly. But I want to encourage you today to believe God that justice will prevail. Not only will the wicked be penalized, but Father God has assured us that the righteous and his descendants will be rewarded.

When we stay connected and submitted to our Father, He promises to make everything right. It may not happen in our timing, but it will come to pass. So if you've been treated unfairly, don't allow yourself to fall into unforgiveness or let bitterness take root, damaging your own soul.[1] Instead, practice blessing your enemies. This will help you guard against developing a vengeful, hateful spirit.

At first, your heart may not be in it, but just speak to the Spirit of God and say, "Lord, I bless my enemy." You don't have to become best friends with the person, but whenever you think about the situation, ask Father God to bless those who hurt you. And then stay in faith, believing God has good plans for you. As you keep your heart pure before Him, the Lord will make all things right for you. Amen!

GOD CONFIDENCE

The Lord is my light and my salvation; whom shall I fear?
The Lord is the defense of my life; whom shall I dread? When
evildoers came upon me to devour my flesh, my adver-
saries and my enemies, they stumbled and fell. Though a
host encamp against me, my heart will not fear; though
war arise against me, in spite of this I shall be confident.
—PSALM 27:1–3

WHAT INCREDIBLE FAVOR David had, and what a
gift it was for him to know the Lord was taking
care of his enemies.

Father God said to Yeshua, "Sit at My right hand,
until I put Your enemies beneath Your feet."[1] I want to
encourage you, beloved one. Don't think you have to
control everything. Rather than looking out and trying
to handle everyone and everything that tries to attack
you, just trust that God is for you. Just focus on having
a right heart toward Him and being in alignment with
HaShem, and watch what He does to those who are
accusing and coming against you. You're going to see
that the Lord is going before you, that He truly is the
defense of your life.

"Neither death, nor life, nor angels, nor principalities,
nor things present, nor things to come, nor powers, nor
height, nor depth, nor any other created thing, will be
able to separate us from the love of God."[2] Father God
is with you. May He impart to you a healthy dose of
"God confidence" today.

Day 80
CLING TO GOD

I came that they may have life, and have it abundantly.
—JOHN 10:10

THAT PROMISE REALLY impacted me when I was young in my faith. I believed Jesus was going to raise me up to a place of victory in the Spirit, where I would have complete peace and freedom in Him. But when I looked at other followers of Yeshua, I did not see the victory I desired. They did not seem to be free or living victoriously. We all go through challenges, but many believers appeared to be beaten down and walking in defeat.

I asked the Lord why so many of His people weren't living an abundant life in Him, and after waiting on Him several days, I clearly sensed the Holy Spirit say, "You are seeing what you are seeing because My people are not trusting Me." As He spoke, the words "trusting Me" burst with new meaning. By "trusting," the Lord meant "clinging."

Beloved one, we must cling to God if we are to have supernatural power to overcome the devil and experience freedom and victory. We can't depend on ourselves; we must fully look to God to lead us, establish us in the Word, and ground us in His Spirit. By clinging to God through difficult times, we are strengthened from within. Eventually, God's Spirit within us will break forth. As we learn to live from the inside out rather than from the outside in, Christ within us will emerge and make us whole.

TELL THE TRUTH, EVEN WHEN IT COSTS YOU

So have I become your enemy by telling you the truth?
—GALATIANS 4:16

THERE IS A price to pay, beloved one, for telling the truth. This is a reality we all must come to grips with.

If our motivation is pure, we cannot allow the fact that the truth may be upsetting to someone stop us from saying it. Our words, though they may sting at first, often will produce positive change in the person's life. When Paul spoke the truth to the saints in Galatia, they turned on him, and we may experience the same thing. This is the price we must be willing to pay if we're going to be truth tellers.

Of course, we must examine our own hearts first. Telling the truth doesn't mean we share everything we think. It means saying what the Holy Spirit, who is the Spirit of Truth, prompts us to speak.

Oftentimes we think we're loving to people by not saying something we think might offend them. But not telling someone the truth is sometimes the least loving thing we could do. Many people don't share the truth of Jesus because they don't want to offend or be rejected. But if Jesus is who He said He is—the Messiah—then the most loving thing we can do is tell people about Him, whether they receive our message or not.

Beloved one, love without truth is not really love, and truth without love is not really truth. Let's be truth tellers.

STILL SMALL VOICE

...and after the earthquake a fire, but the LORD was
not in the fire; and after the fire a still small voice.
—1 KINGS 19:12, NKJV

IN REVELATION 2, Jesus said: "The one who has an ear, let him hear what the Spirit says to the churches."[1] Obviously, Yeshua is saying: "When you hear the Spirit speaking, listen." To hear the Holy Spirit we must be actively listening.

To detect the Holy Spirit's voice, we need to develop the art of *intuitive listening*. A practical way to develop this sensitivity to the Spirit's leading is to begin each day by spending alone time with God. During this time we simply look up, sit quietly before Him, and know that He is God. I often listen to gentle worship music during this devotional time.

Beloved one, if we are not disciplining ourselves by sitting before Him and simply being still, we will miss so many of the benefits of being His children. The prophet Elijah said the Lord spoke in a "still small voice." Detecting the Holy Spirit's voice is an intentional and trained behavior. It requires such a keen awareness that if we have not developed our attentiveness—if we are not actively listening—we can miss Him.

I want to encourage you today. In order to walk in divine alignment with the Lord and live under His anointing, it will take spiritual discipline. This will then produce active listening that will enable you to hear His still small voice.

GO ALL IN

If it is disagreeable in your sight to serve the Lord,
choose for yourselves today whom you will serve...but
as for me and my house, we will serve the Lord.
—Joshua 24:15

THERE IS NO middle ground in God. Like the Israelites of old, we must chose who we're going to follow: either God or the world. We can't serve both. If we're going to follow the Lord, we must take our stand, realizing that may mean being rejected for the cause of Christ. We must be His light in the earth, even if it hurts.

Those who want to be accepted by the world can choose the world. They can adopt the posture of the ungodly and reap the consequences. But if we say we're choosing the Lord, then let's do it! Let's live like we belong to Him. Let's cleanse ourselves of the things that defile us so we'll be useful to the Master and prepared for every good work. There is no room for compromise. Jesus spits the lukewarm out of His mouth.[1]

Yeshua said straight and narrow is the way that leads to life, and few there be that find it, but broad and wide is the way that leads to destruction, and many there be that take it.[2] Yeshua chose the Father and was crucified for it. Will you give your time, talent, and treasure to Him first? Beloved one, if we say we choose the Lord, let's go all in.

Day 84

HOW GOD SEES YOU

For you are all sons [and daughters] of
God through faith in Christ Jesus.
—GALATIANS 3:26

HAVE YOU EVER thought about the incredible truth that you are a child of God? For a lot of us, it's easier to accept that Jesus died on the cross to forgive our sins than to believe we are God's children. But the reality is that just as earthly parents are proud of their children and focus their love on them, so does our heavenly Father delight in us.

Because of Jesus, sin—the barrier that separated us from God—is gone forever, and we now are holy and blameless in Him. He now sees us as brand new, having all of our past failures erased by Yeshua's blood. "The Spirit himself bears witness with our spirit that we are the children of God."[1] So when the Lord looks at you, He does not see you as a sinful person; Jesus took away your sins. Now, Father looks at you as His beloved child whom He continually delights in.

Just like any earthly father who loves his child, our heavenly Father may discipline us at times, but this does not change His love for us. Father God will always have our best interest at heart.

Beloved one, let's get our identity from the One who gave His life for us. I want to encourage you to receive this truth today: you are God's child, your Father delights in you, and His plans for you are far greater than anything you could imagine.

A SURRENDERED LIFE

Have this attitude in yourselves which was also in Christ
Jesus, who, although He existed in the form of God...emp-
tied Himself, taking the form of a bond-servant, and...
humbled Himself by becoming obedient to the point of death.
—PHILIPPIANS 2:5–8

JESUS GAVE UP His own will, His own desires, His own rights in order to serve the Father. This call is the call on our lives as well. God is asking you and me to give up our personal interests to put Him first.

Beloved one, we do not belong to ourselves. Too many of us think we're in this world to fulfill ourselves or simply enjoy life. But we have been called to put on the mind of Christ. We want to develop the mindset of Jesus, who humbly took on the form of a servant and obeyed His Father even to the point of death. As a result, "God highly exalted Him, and bestowed on Him the name which is above every name, so that at the name of Jesus every knee will bow...and that every tongue will confess that Jesus Christ is Lord."[1]

Jesus said to the Father, "Not My will, but Yours be done."[2] Will you do the same? Will you give up your rights, desires, and preferences and instead say yes to the Father and follow Him? There's a great reward for those of us who will put our own desires under our feet and choose to obey Him instead.

TAKING OUR THOUGHTS CAPTIVE

*We are destroying speculations and every lofty thing
raised up against the knowledge of God, and we are
taking every thought captive to the obedience of Christ.*
—2 CORINTHIANS 10:5

WHAT ARE THE speculations and lofty things Paul is referring to in today's verse? He's talking about spiritual warfare in the realm of our thoughts. This is the territory of the enemy. The enemy moves in the realm of thought. Even before words are spoken, there are thoughts. Words just give verbal expression to thoughts. So the base level for spiritual warfare is the level of the mind.

God wants you and me to become so alive in our self-awareness and so strong in our spirit that we're monitoring every thought that is presented to us and casting down every thought of worry, terror, deception, distraction, lust, or inferiority. Every single thought that comes at us that is from the realm of darkness, Messiah Jesus wants us to challenge it, take hold of it, and cast it down.

Beloved one, I speak over you right now a supernatural divine impartation by the living Word of God through the Ruach HaKodesh to wake up, pick up the weapons of warfare, and fight to tear off you every thought that is exalting itself above the Lordship of Messiah Yeshua. As you do, you will ascend to reign in Christ Jesus and live in the courage and confidence that has been ordained for you. It's time to be free in the battleground of our minds.

BE STRONG AND COURAGEOUS

Have I not commanded you? Be strong and cou-
rageous! Do not tremble or be dismayed, for the
LORD your God is with you wherever you go.
—JOSHUA 1:9

THIS VERSE ISN'T just for our inspiration; it's a command! We are to be strong and courageous.

I know some people see themselves as naturally timid, but that's no excuse to disobey God. The Bible says, "God has not given us a spirit of fear, but of power and of love and of a sound mind."[1] We need to get on the same page with God and stop accepting natural dispositions that aren't in alignment with who He has called us to be. We need to fight the good fight of faith, breaking the power of intimidation. We are called and commanded to step into a posture of strength.

I know this is easier said than done, but we can't give the devil any room in our lives or make excuses for what God hates. We all struggle with fear, myself included. But the Lord is calling us to crush fear under our feet and be transformed into bold, confident people who are full of faith. This won't happen all at once. It's a process. But as we refuse to listen to the devil's lies, we will progressively move from strength to strength.

Beloved one, there's a banner of victory over us. Let's fight each day. Then instead of running from the devil, he'll be running from us! The hunted will become the hunter.

THE CHOICE IS YOURS

Therefore if you have been raised up with Christ, keep seeking the things above, where Christ is, seated at the right hand of God. Set your mind on the things above, not on the things that are on earth.

—COLOSSIANS 3:1–2

IT'S UNFORTUNATE THAT many who claim to be followers of Yeshua are not seeking first the things that are above. Yeshua has been raised up to the right hand of God and is seated there in heavenly places, but many believers are craving the things of the earth. Seeking to fulfill the longing of our souls with the pleasures of this world instead of with knowing Messiah is a horrendously foul, demonic deception.

Please consider what you are giving yourself to today. What are you directing most of your energy toward? Are you taking time to sit alone with God, examine your thoughts, and pray? "Watch over your heart with all diligence, for from it flow the springs of life."[1] Are you separating yourself unto the Lord so He can fill you with Himself? Or are you spending all your time on social media, watching TV, shopping, or talking to your earthly friends? We must put God first.

The Lord will not force us to choose Him; rather, He said, "I have set before you life and death....Choose life in order that you may live."[2] Yeshua said He is the way, the truth, and the life. The choice is yours.

NO GREATER INHERITANCE

And if children, heirs also, heirs of God
and fellow heirs with Christ.
—ROMANS 8:17

GOD DOES NOT just put up with you—He loves and delights in you. Father celebrates you. He rejoices over you with singing, and His banner over you is love because you are His child.

Today's verse reveals what a glorious privilege we have. We are heirs of God. That means God Himself is our inheritance, and He has given us His Spirit as a pledge of our inheritance.[1] What could we want that is greater than God Himself? In Him is fullness of joy, peace, contentment, and satisfaction. Life consists not in the abundance of material things obtained; real life is found in the Holy Spirit. We have been made heirs of God. The fullness of life, joy, glory, happiness, power, and identity—they are all ours in Him!

There is no greater inheritance than the inheritance of God Himself. He is our victory! As we learn to be led by the Holy Spirit, we not only receive His guidance to help us navigate this life, but we also experience the reality that we are the sons and daughters of Father God. And if we are children of God, then we are heirs of God! I want to encourage you to walk as a child of the Creator of the universe and pursue your inheritance—God Himself. We are on a journey and a quest!

Day 90

TRUST HIM AND OPEN THE DOOR

And those who know Your name will put their trust in You,
for You, LORD, have not abandoned those who seek You.
—PSALM 9:10

WHEN WE FULLY depend upon the Lord, His grace comes in and strengthens us. His "power is perfected in weakness."[1] Our temporary struggles can become a platform for future momentum and breakthrough!

Our problems are God's opportunities. Yet when dealing with something, we may become so anxious and fearful that we shut off honest communion with Father. Instead, we should cling to God in our challenges, exhibiting trust that the trial can become a gift. As we cling to Father in the midst of our problems, not only will we overcome them—we will be better because of them.

Paul told the church in Corinth he faced such hardship that he despaired even of life. "Indeed, we had the sentence of death within ourselves so that we would not trust in ourselves, but in God who raises the dead."[2] Paul was saying, "The Lord put me in such a place of hardship and weakness that there was no natural solution for me and the only thing left for me to do was look up and connect with God, who raises the dead."

Will you break away from looking for man to be your answer? God is knocking at the door of your heart right now. He is waiting for you to let Him in. Let's put all our confidence in Him!

Day 91

A PROMISE TO CLING TO

Neither height nor depth, nor any other cre-
ated thing, shall be able to separate us from the
love of God, which is in Christ Jesus our Lord.
—ROMANS 8:39, MEV

THERE ARE PEOPLE who read the Scriptures and take promises given to specific people in particular circumstances and apply them to themselves. Not all promises in God's Word are meant to be applied to all people at all times. But there are certain promises in Scripture that we can apply to ourselves and cling to. Today's verse is one of them.

I don't know about you, but life is often a mystery to me. I face seasons I don't understand, and sometimes it can feel like no-man's-land. But the promise in God's Word is that regardless of what we're experiencing now or what we'll face in the future, nothing will ever be able to separate us from the love of God.

At times we may feel like we're disconnected from God's love, but that doesn't mean we actually are. Feelings come and go and are not facts. Facts are defined by the Word of God. "The grass withers, the flower fades, but the word of our God stands forever."[1] Beloved one, God loves you, and His love will never fail you. He has you safely in His arms, and He's going to carry you all the way through this life, and then into His bosom in the very end.

DIVINE SATISFACTION

*Ask, and it will be given to you; seek, and you
will find; knock, and it will be opened to you. For
everyone who asks receives, and he who seeks
finds, and to him who knocks it will be opened.*
—MATTHEW 7:7–8

IF WE REALLY believe the Lord answers those who call
out to Him, we're going to pursue Him. If we truly
trust that if we draw near to Father, He'll draw near to
us, we're going to reach out to Him expecting Him to
reward us.[1]

And what reward should we anticipate? Yeshua said,
"This is eternal life, that they may know You, the only
true God, and Jesus Christ whom You have sent."[2] The
greatest reward is to have our soul satisfied by truly
knowing who God is. I'm talking about having a deep,
abiding inner peace because we sought Father God and
He brought our souls into alignment with Himself. I'm
talking about coming to a place in Yeshua where we feel
embraced, safe, and loved. And because we know we're
loved, we have confidence, which makes us happy.

Yeshua said, "He who believes in Me…'From his
innermost being will flow rivers of living water.'"[3]
Beloved one, this is more satisfying than anything the
world can fill us with. Amen? Let's seek Father for the
greatest thing of all: to know Him and who we are to
Him. In discovering Him, we will find a well of living
water so we will thirst no more.[4]

STAND IN THE MIDST
OF DARKNESS

For the mystery of lawlessness is already at work; only he
who now restrains will do so until he is taken out of the way.
—2 THESSALONIANS 2:7

THE REASON WE are seeing such chaos and confusion in the world is because as we move deeper into the last days, God is going to begin to stop exerting the same amount of His authority and government in the world. This will create the environment for the Antichrist to arise, which the Scriptures teach must happen before Jesus returns.[1]

As the Holy Spirit begins to pull back, evil is going to rise, and that is what we're dealing with right now. We feel it in the culture. We feel it in politics. We see it in the brokenness of relationships. All over, we see that chaos and evil are having sway.

These are serious times, and in order to stand, we need to seek the Lord more unreservedly and passionately than ever. We must feed ourselves daily with the Word and talk to God all day long, even if it's silently. Seize His Word, beloved one, and don't let anything else in. As you do, as the times gets darker, you will continue to move forward in the Lord, and you will stand. Even in the end times, you "will be like a tree firmly planted by streams of water, which yields its fruit in its season and its leaf does not wither; and in whatever he does, he prospers."[2]

Day 94

FAITH THAT MOVES MOUNTAINS

Truly I say to you, whoever says to this moun-
tain, "Be taken up and cast into the sea," and does
not doubt in his heart, but believes that what he
says is going to happen, it will be granted him.
—MARK 11:23

FAITH IS POWERFUL, but we have to war for it. Doubt takes no effort, but faith takes *kavanah*—it takes focus and intention. Believing is like paddling against the current; we must fight for it. Yet Yeshua said, "If you believe, you will see the glory of God."[1] So to see God's glory manifest in our lives, we must believe. There is no other way.

But what should we believe? We should believe God is good. We should believe Father wants to bless us and will do so. We should believe we are protected in Him. We should believe God is at work in our lives "both to will and to work for His good pleasure."[2]

I want to encourage you to stand in faith. Yeshua said, "This is the work of God, that you believe in Him whom He has sent."[3] Beloved one, we don't have to labor for the answers to our prayers. We don't have to pray louder or try harder to receive from the Lord. All we need to do is believe that God has heard the whisper of our hearts and that we have what we've requested. This is how we build faith that can move mountains.

Day 95

PAY ATTENTION

He who has an ear, let him hear what
the Spirit says to the churches.
—REVELATION 2:29

ALTHOUGH FATHER GOD fundamentally has spoken to us through His written Word, He can also speak through our circumstances. This is why we should always pay attention.

I have a friend who was reading from the Book of Isaiah, and Isaiah 40:31 just popped out at him: "Those who wait for the Lord will gain new strength; they will mount up with wings like eagles." When he read that verse, he felt the Lord wanted him to share it with me but wasn't completely sure it was the Lord leading him.

Suddenly, a woman whose last name was Schneider walked into the room where he was, wearing a T-shirt with an eagle on it! He knew what to do. He called and told me about the scripture. I was encouraged by it, but I didn't know what was personal about it for me since it is a very well-known verse.

A few days later I looked out my window and saw a real, live bald eagle sitting on a tree stump in my backyard! I'd never seen one that close, and it blew me away. I knew God was encouraging me to be patient in hope and expectation of what He was about to do in my life.

Beloved one, I hope this encourages us all to know that God is at work in the circumstances of our lives as we seek Him. Let's all be paying attention.

Day 96

COMPLETELY SELL OUT

For to everyone who has, more shall be given, and he
will have an abundance; but from the one who does not
have, even what he does have shall be taken away.
—MATTHEW 25:29

IN THE PARABLE of the Talents in Matthew 25, the talents represent the ability God has given us to bless others and build His kingdom. God dictates the talents one is born with, but we determine what we do with them. In other words, God defines the amount each of us is given, but we determine how much we increase those talents, whether thirtyfold, sixtyfold, or a hundredfold.[1]

Many of us desire to be found faithful and please our heavenly Father. But just because we want to multiply our talents a hundredfold does not mean we will do it. "The spirit is willing, but the flesh is weak."[2] If we are going to multiply what God has given us, we must make a conscious decision to sell out to Jesus by letting go of everything and completely surrendering to God.

I remember hearing a preacher share a story about a time when the Lord commissioned him to do something. As he was on his knees, he said, "Yes, Lord, I will do it." And the Lord spoke to him clearly and said, "Many have said they would do it, but none did."

Beloved one, you are in control of your will. Do not pass off on God what He is calling you to do. Too many of us say, "Well, whatever God wills." Sometimes it's not about what God wills but about what you and I will choose to do. To bear a hundredfold fruit, we must completely sell out.

THE RESURRECTION IS PROOF

*He appeared to Cephas, then to the twelve. After
that He appeared to more than five hundred
brethren at one time....and last of all, as to one
untimely born, He appeared to me also.*
—1 Corinthians 15:5–6, 8

THE RESURRECTION OF Jesus is a historical fact and
the foundation of our faith. Everything flows from
this. Without this reality we would still be lost in our
sins and without hope.

The resurrection of Jesus became the overwhelming
evidence that ignited Paul to declare without hesitation
that Yeshua is the way to God. Thus, the gospel Paul
preached was not some fluffy, politically correct message; rather, he boldly proclaimed that not all paths lead
to the same place. Unfortunately, many today believe
that anyone who tries to be a nice person will go to
heaven.

In the days to come, it will become increasingly contro-
versial to insist that Jesus is the only way to enter heaven
and to cleave to His Word: "I am the way, and the truth,
and the life; no one comes to the Father but through
Me."[1] Paul and many others gave their lives for this message. We need to stake our lives on the historical fact that
God rescued Jesus from the grave and He is alive!

The resurrection of Jesus echoes throughout history with a loud and distinguishing sound of victory.
Yeshua's resurrection has provided the ultimate way for
us to overcome the world and the grave.

A VISION OF FREEDOM

Through Him everyone who believes is freed from all things,
from which you could not be freed through the Law of Moses.
—ACTS 13:39

THE EXODUS STORY contains symbolism that is very relevant for us today. God's people, Israel, were living in captivity in Egypt, oppressed by the powers of darkness forced upon them through Pharaoh. Pharaoh intended to do only one thing, and that was to subject God's people to slavery.

Similarly, you and I, as God's people today, find ourselves oppressed by the powers of darkness. Satan has one thing intended for us: to take us captive and separate us from the freedom Jesus brings. But just as ancient Israel was delivered by God through the blood of a lamb at Passover, we have been redeemed by the blood of Yeshua—the ultimate and eternal Lamb of God.

God intervened in the lives of His chosen people, freeing them and bringing them to Himself. And Father has the same intent for us. He wants us to be free, victorious, joyful, and filled with supernatural peace. Although you may be struggling right now, I want you to know God has planned something greater for you, and it will make all your sorrows disappear.

The freedom Father is bringing us into doesn't happen all at once. God is driving out our enemies little by little, just as He did for Israel. As we stay the course, we will continue to make progress toward the ultimate goal— the freedom of God Himself!

Day 99

STAY HUNGRY

*Call to Me and I will answer you, and I will tell you
great and mighty things, which you do not know.*
—Jeremiah 33:3

D O YOU HUNGER for more? Do you want the Lord to reveal to you new dimensions of His glory? Do you want a life filled with adventure? This is what Father God is promising in today's verse. He's promising that as we keep seeking Him—as we keep knocking, asking, and calling on Him—He's going to cause the glory of heaven to come upon our lives, and He's going to reveal Himself to us in ways we've never experienced! Amen.

I know sometimes life seems dry. It seems monotonous and mechanical. But we have to go through these times. God is working in our lives even when we're in the midst of the valley or it seems as if nothing is happening, just as He's working in the trees during the winter when all their leaves are gone. In fact, trees can better soak up nutrients in the winter when they don't have to spread that nourishment to the outer leaves. In much the same way, God is working in your life even during those dry winter seasons when you don't feel His presence.

There's a time for everything, and the Lord says if you call upon Him, He's going to reveal His glory to you in ways you've never known. Beloved one, I want to encourage you to stay hungry and expectant. Don't give up hope. Keep pressing on. God is alive. There's more for you.

YOU ARE AN OVERCOMER

*These things I have spoken to you, so that in Me
you may have peace. In the world you have tribulation, but take courage; I have overcome the world.*
—JOHN 16:33

G OD NEVER PROMISED that we wouldn't face hard
times. In fact, the opposite is true. Jesus said in the
world we will have trouble. But He went on to say we
should be of good cheer, for He has overcome the world.

Some of us are trying to be of good cheer by con-
trolling everything, thinking we can protect ourselves
from life's difficulties, but that's not possible because we
live in a world full of darkness and chaos. While Jesus
never promised we wouldn't face hardship, what He did
promise is that we will overcome every battle we'll ever
have to face. And not only that, but we'll *"overwhelmingly conquer* through Him who loved us."[1]

That means you're not going to just get through.
You're not going to just survive and grit your teeth and
hope for the best. You're going to be overwhelmingly
victorious in every struggle and difficulty. We might
not feel triumphant in the moment, but those who truly
have set their minds on Christ Jesus will be able to look
back on their lives and see that God used everything
they went through for good. Beloved one, at the end of
the day, we are going to transcend every obstacle. Our
lives carry the sweet aroma of the victory of Messiah
Yeshua.[2]

If you enjoyed this book and believe other people would be helped by reading it, please leave a review on Amazon.

NOTES

INTRODUCTION

1. John 4:14.
2. John 4:23–24.
3. John 7:38.

CHAPTER 1

1. Elizabeth Hopper, PhD, "The Study of Authenticity (Positive Psychology Series #3)," HealthyPsych, February 12, 2018, https://healthypsych.com/the-study-of-authenticity/.
2. Matthew 15:8.
3. Romans 5:8.
4. Hebrews 4:16.
5. Genesis 2:16–17; 3:1–8.
6. Ephesians 1:6, NKJV.
7. 2 Corinthians 12:9.
8. 2 Corinthians 12:7.
9. 2 Corinthians 12:8–9.
10. 1 Thessalonians 5:17.
11. 2 Corinthians 1:8.
12. 2 Corinthians 1:9.
13. Revelation 3:20.
14. John 11:41–42, emphasis added.
15. 1 Corinthians 5:17.
16. Deuteronomy 30:12–14.
17. Romans 10:6–8.

CHAPTER 2

1. Matthew 22:41–45.
2. Psalm 51:1–10.
3. See Romans 1:7, 1 Corinthians 1:3, 2 Corinthians 1:2, Galatians 1:3, Ephesians 1:2, Philippians 1:2, Colossians 1:2, 1 Thessalonians 1:1, 2 Thessalonians 1:2, 1 Timothy 1:2, 2 Timothy 1:2, Titus 1:4, and Philemon 3.
4. Ephesians 1:6, NKJV.
5. 1 Timothy 1:15.
6. 1 Timothy 1:12–16.
7. 1 Timothy 1:15.
8. Hebrews 4:16.
9. Psalm 51:1.

10. Psalm 103:10–11.
11. Leviticus 17:11.
12. Ephesians 1:3.
13. Romans 7:18–20, 24–25.
14. See Matthew 6:5.
15. Exodus 25:8.
16. Exodus 25:9.
17. Isaiah 55:8–9.
18. See Psalm 141:2, and Revelation 5:8 and 8:3–4.
19. Psalm 51:4.

Chapter 3

1. Psalm 51:1–10.
2. Psalm 46:10, NIV.
3. Psalm 131:2.
4. Jamie Waters, "Constant Craving: How Digital Media Turned Us All Into Dopamine Addicts," *The Guardian*, August 22, 2021, https://www.theguardian.com/global/2021/aug/22/how-digital-media-turned-us-all-into-dopamine-addicts-and-what-we-can-do-to-break-the-cycle; Trevor Haynes, "Dopamine, Smartphones and You: A Battle for Your Time," Harvard University, May 1, 2018, https://sitn.hms.harvard.edu/flash/2018/dopamine-smartphones-battle-time/.
5. Erika Edwards, "Social Media Use Linked to Depression in Adults," NBC News, November 23, 2021, https://www.nbcnews.com/health/health-news/social-media-use-linked-depression-adults-rcna6445.
6. Jeremiah 2:13.
7. 1 John 2:16.
8. Colossians 1:26–27.
9. John 4:14.
10. Matthew 6:6.
11. John 7:38.
12. Ecclesiastes 3:11.
13. Ephesians 1:18, NKJV, emphasis added.
14. Matthew 16:25.
15. Matthew 16:24.
16. Psalm 51:6.
17. Proverbs 1:20–23.

18. John 3:6–7.
19. 1 Timothy 4:7–8.
20. Philippians 3:12, 14.
21. James 3:2–10.
22. Psalm 51:7–8.
23. Psalm 51:8.
24. Psalm 51:10.
25. Philippians 1:6.
26. Titus 3:5.
27. Psalm 19:14.
28. See Romans 7:14–25.
29. Revelation 2:7.
30. Revelation 22:12.

CHAPTER 4

1. Mark 11:24.
2. Ephesians 3:16–17.
3. Colossians 2:10.
4. Luke 17:21, KJV.
5. Colossians 1:25–27, emphasis added.
6. Ephesians 3:14, 16–17.
7. Ephesians 3:17.
8. Matthew 16:13–18.
9. Matthew 16:16.
10. Matthew 16:17–18.
11. John 6:45.
12. Matthew 11:29, KJV.
13. John 11:21–26, emphasis added.
14. John 15:7.
15. John 15:12, 16–17.
16. Ephesians 3:18.
17. Ephesians 3:19, emphasis added.
18. Ephesians 3:18–19.
19. Jeremiah 2:13.
20. Ephesians 3:20.
21. 1 Corinthians 2:9, NKJV.

CHAPTER 5

1. John 1:12; 5:24; Romans 6:23.
2. John 17:3, emphasis added.

3. John 10:10.
4. John 8:36.
5. John 4:9–14.
6. 1 John 2:16.
7. Psalm 1:3.
8. Ephesians 1:18.
9. John 14:27.
10. John 15:11.
11. 1 Corinthians 2:16.
12. John 13:3.
13. Ephesians 1:3.
14. Luke 3:21–22.
15. Matthew 3:17.
16. John 4:31–33.
17. John 13:3.
18. 1 Peter 1:4–5.
19. Luke 10:20.
20. 1 John 5:13.
21. Romans 8:28.
22. Colossians 3:1–3.
23. Matthew 6:33.
24. Romans 8:29.
25. John 4:34.
26. Matthew 6:9–10.
27. 1 John 5:14–15, emphasis added.
28. Luke 22:42.

Chapter 6

1. Genesis 5:24.
2. Matthew 16:26.
3. See Job 2:10.
4. Hebrews 12:6.
5. 2 Corinthians 12:7.
6. See 2 Corinthians 12:9.
7. Revelation 21:7.
8. Revelation 2:7, 11, 17, 29; 3:6, 13, 22.
9. John 1:1.
10. See Luke 3:2 and Ezekiel 1:28.
11. Job 33:14–15.
12. Genesis 28:10–17.

13. Galatians 5:22–23.
14. Galatians 5:19–21.
15. Galatians 3:27.
16. Colossians 3:12.
17. Matthew 7:13–14.
18. James 1:3, AMP.
19. Romans 8:29.
20. Ephesians 1:4.
21. Genesis 15:1, NKJV.
22. Romans 8:1, MEV.
23. Romans 8:38–39.
24. Revelation 19:9.
25. Revelation 3:20.

CHAPTER 7

1. Job 33:15.
2. John 17:3.
3. Philippians 3:20.
4. Isaiah 40:8.
5. Psalm 36:9.
6. 2 Corinthians 4:16–18.
7. 1 John 2:16.
8. 1 Peter 2:11.
9. 2 Peter 3:7.
10. Matthew 20:16.
11. Hebrews 11:24–26.
12. Revelation 2:7.
13. 2 Timothy 3:12.
14. Philippians 3:7–8.
15. Matthew 7:22–23.
16. Philippians 1:21.
17. Revelation 22:12.
18. Matthew 6:2–4.
19. Matthew 10:42; Mark 9:41.
20. Deuteronomy 6:4, CJB.
21. Deuteronomy 6:4.
22. See John 16:13–15.
23. John 6:63.

DAY 2

1. Luke 4:21.
2. John 8:32, 36.
3. "The Westminster Shorter Catechism," The Presbytery of the United States, accessed September 20, 2022, https://www.westminsterconfession.org/resources/confessional-standards/the-westminster-shorter-catechism/.

DAY 4

1. 1 John 5:4.

DAY 6

1. Psalm 37:24.

DAY 7

1. Exodus 3:1–3.
2. Exodus 7:11.

DAY 8

1. 1 Corinthians 2:9.

DAY 9

1. John 15:5.
2. Romans 16:20.

DAY 11

1. 2 Corinthians 12:9.

DAY 12

1. Ephesians 4:7.

DAY 13

1. John 3:36.
2. Matthew 7:13.

DAY 15

1. Nehemiah 8:10.
2. Romans 8:28.

DAY 16

1. John 4:10–14.

DAY 17

1. Ephesians 2:8–9.
2. 2 Corinthians 13:5.

DAY 19

1. 2 Timothy 3:12.

DAY 21

1. Genesis 15:1, KJV.

DAY 23

1. Ephesians 1:4.
2. Revelation 3:21.
3. Isaiah 49:23.

DAY 24

1. 1 Chronicles 14:11.
2. Ecclesiastes 3:11, KJV.

DAY 25

1. Luke 17:17.

DAY 26

1. Hebrews 12:2.
2. Titus 3:5.
3. Ephesians 2:8.
4. 2 Timothy 2:13.

DAY 28

1. 1 Thessalonians 4:16–17.
2. Revelation 22:20.
3. Revelation 22:12.
4. 1 Corinthians 15:52.

DAY 30

1. Genesis 6:9–22.
2. Matthew 9:36.
3. Psalm 103:13–14.

DAY 33

1. Philippians 4:13.

DAY 34

1. Matthew 10:39.

DAY 35

1. Ephesians 3:20.
2. Revelation 12:10.

DAY 36

1. Psalm 5:3.
2. 1 Chronicles 23:30.
3. 1 Peter 2:9.

DAY 37

1. Colossians 2:10.

DAY 39

1. Matthew 6:9.
2. John 14:6.
3. Romans 11:36.

DAY 40

1. 2 Corinthians 4:17.

DAY 42

1. Exodus 29:34–35.

DAY 43

1. Romans 8:35, 37.

DAY 44

1. Hebrews 11:10.
2. Revelation 22:12.

DAY 45

1. John 15:15.

DAY 46

1. Luke 22:19–20.

DAY 47

1. John 15:19.
2. 2 Timothy 3:12.

3. Matthew 5:10.

DAY 51

1. Ephesians 6:12.
2. Matthew 4:1.
3. Revelation 2:10.

DAY 52

1. John 10:10.
2. Psalm 84:11.

DAY 53

1. Mark 8:34, KJV.

DAY 55

1. Matthew 10:42.
2. 1 Corinthians 16:13.

DAY 56

1. 1 John 3:8.

DAY 57

1. Psalm 19:9.
2. Isaiah 11:2.
3. Matthew 10:28.

DAY 58

1. John 6:63.

DAY 59

1. 2 Corinthians 4:16.

DAY 60

1. Isaiah 55:9.

DAY 61

1. Acts 1:8.
2. 2 Corinthians 5:20.

DAY 63

1. Deuteronomy 30:19.

DAY 64

1. 2 Peter 1:3.

DAY 65

1. James 4:6, KJV.

DAY 66

1. Romans 1:20.
2. Jeremiah 29:13.

DAY 67

1. Psalm 92:12–14.

DAY 68

1. John 11:34–35.
2. Isaiah 66:2.
3. Matthew 18:44.

DAY 69

1. Hebrews 5:14.

DAY 70

1. Romans 11:17, 24.
2. Ephesians 2:13.

DAY 71

1. John 20:21.

DAY 72

1. Matthew 24:25–26.
2. Matthew 19:21.

DAY 73

1. Ephesians 6:17.

DAY 75

1. Matthew 13:12.

DAY 76

1. Matthew 10:37.

DAY 77

1. Genesis 18:10.
2. 2 Corinthians 5:7.

DAY 78

1. Hebrews 12:15.

DAY 79

1. Matthew 22:44.
2. Romans 8:38–39.

DAY 82

1. Revelation 2:29.

DAY 83

1. Revelation 3:16.
2. Matthew 7:13–14.

DAY 84

1. Romans 8:16.

DAY 85

1. Philippians 2:9–11.
2. Luke 22:42.

DAY 87

1. 2 Timothy 1:7, NKJV.

DAY 88

1. Proverbs 4:23.
2. Deuteronomy 30:19.

DAY 89

1. Ephesians 1:13–14.

DAY 90

1. 2 Corinthians 12:9.
2. 2 Corinthians 1:9.

DAY 91

1. Isaiah 40:8.

DAY 92

1. Hebrews 11:6.
2. John 17:3.
3. John 7:38.
4. John 4:13–15.

DAY 93

1. 2 Thessalonians 2:3.
2. Psalm 1:3.

DAY 94

1. John 11:40.
2. Philippians 2:13.
3. John 6:29.

DAY 96

1. Matthew 13:8.
2. Matthew 26:41.

DAY 97

1. John 14:6.

DAY 100

1. Romans 8:37, emphasis added.
2. 2 Corinthians 2:15.

DISCOVERING THE JEWISH JESUS

CONNECT WITH RABBI SCHNEIDER

www.DiscoveringTheJewishJesus.com

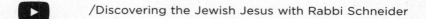 /Discovering the Jewish Jesus with Rabbi Schneider

facebook.com/rabbischneider

@RabbiSchneider

Roku—Discovering the Jewish Jesus

Apple TV—Discovering the Jewish Jesus

Amazon App—Discovering the Jewish Jesus

Podcast—Discovering the Jewish Jesus

Search for Rabbi Schneider and Discovering the Jewish Jesus on your favorite platform.

For a complete list of Rabbi Schneider's television and radio broadcasts, visit www.DiscoveringTheJewishJesus.com.